What's It Like?

Life and Culture in Britain Today

Teacher's Book

JOANNE COLLIE
& ALEX MARTIN

CAMBRIDGE
UNIVERSITY PRESS

CAMBRIDGE UNIVERSITY PRESS
Cambridge, New York, Melbourne, Madrid, Cape Town, Singapore, São Paulo, Delhi

Cambridge University Press
The Edinburgh Building, Cambridge CB2 8RU, UK

www.cambridge.org
Information on this title: www.cambridge.org/9780521586610

First published 2000
5th printing 2008

Printed in the United Kingdom at the University Press, Cambridge

A catalogue record for this publication is available from the British Library

ISBN 978-0-521-58661-0 Teacher's Book
ISBN 978-0-521-58662-7 Student's Book
ISBN 978-0-521-58660-3 Cassette

CONTENTS

3

INTRODUCTION

What's It Like? sets out to give a sense of what life is like in Britain today, especially for young adults. The aim is to develop a creative approach to British cultural studies, integrating three areas of socio-cultural and linguistic competence: language as communication, information about society, and finally 'interpretation of life'. Culture is sometimes interpreted as the 'high achievement' of a society, embodied in its literature, its music and its arts; but in this book, culture is also taken in its broader sociological sense of the values and relationships that give meaning to the ordinary facts of everyday life in any given time and social situation. In this sense, of course, it is vitally connected with language. Increasingly, language teachers are recognising the importance of social context in shaping the communicative or performative force of any utterance, and the importance, therefore, of considering it not as 'background' but as an integral part of language learning.

This book is intended for intermediate to upper-intermediate learners of English, although it can also be used at advanced level. Having acquired the basic structures of the language, students need to work through as wide a range of materials and contexts as possible in order to extend their own understanding and appreciation of the full communicative potential of their new language.

The units are not centred on specific language points, but in each one, students are invited to interact with each other in activities designed to make them aware of the context of current British usage and at the same time extend their own language skills. They are asked, for example, to read and consider critically a great variety of authentic texts, amongst them literary works, newspaper articles, government statistics, extracts from brochures or guide books; to listen to unscripted interviews featuring speakers from many backgrounds and walks of life; to produce oral or written assessments of the material, as well as more personal, creative responses to it. The study of a country's culture rests to some extent on knowledge of its history and traditions and it is not surprising, therefore, that it has in the past often meant fact-based surveys of 'life and institutions'. Rather than attempting a comprehensive examination of the entire field of British cultural studies, this book uses its selected themes to provide snapshots of life and experience in contemporary Britain. Hence our title: *What's It Like?* It is hoped that working extensively and more personally with a small number of topics will help learners to develop a productive awareness of the complex issues involved in thinking about culture. In all the units, students are asked to engage with literary or imaginative texts as well as with factual ones; creative response is encouraged and balanced with analysis, providing complementary ways of achieving deeper understanding. Looking closely at another culture often acts as a curious two-way mirror: it makes us aware of what seemed 'transparent', through familiarity, in our own culture. Habits or customs previously accepted in an unexamined way as normal, 'obviously' based on common sense, are suddenly seen in a new light: they are seen as particular rather than universal, and largely shaped by a set of historical and social circumstances. It is this which gives cultural studies its wider educational value as well as its motivating quality. The approach adopted in this book is therefore to take the familiar as a departure point and consistently encourage a comparative, cross-cultural view as students move into less familiar terrain.

WHAT IS BRITAIN?

- To let students call upon and share whatever previous knowledge they have of Britain
- To encourage critical awareness of traditional views and stereotyping
- To introduce concepts of change and variety in the life of Britain and their own country

GENERAL REMARKS

One of the main facts about Britain is that it is not a single nation but four: England, Wales, Scotland, and Northern Ireland. 'Britain', strictly speaking, refers to the first three of these, but the term is often used for simplicity and convenience to refer to the whole of the United Kingdom; for example, the two terms are used interchangeably in the article from *The Guardian* newspaper, *Spoken in the UK*, on page 12 of this unit. 'Britain' and 'British' are quite often used in this way throughout the book.

The four countries are marked by many individual characteristics, which means that lifestyles, language, accent, and traditions can vary to a considerable extent from one to the other. In addition, the main island is criss-crossed by regional divisions, some of them based upon the administrative units that are its counties, some on long historical traditions, and others representing simply the differences people feel if they are living in, for example, the North as opposed to the South, or East Anglia as opposed to London.

In this first unit, students explore a few of these broad regional variations and gain some idea of the great diversity of life and cultures in various parts of Britain. They are invited to build on what they already know about Britain, and consider similarities and differences with their own country.

A BRITAIN AND THE BRITISH

A brainstorming exercise. Students write down their items individually, then compare and categorise them together, on the board. The final question invites feedback: Have students in your class been to any of the four countries? What was their experience? Is there any one country they don't know very well at all? Perhaps others in the class can give them more information about it. Is there one which they find particularly attractive, in which case they can share their interest with others? If it is possible, a class list is kept of the items (or students can keep individual lists) and further details are added to it as students work through the unit. This can then lead in to the Follow-up project that is suggested at the end of this unit.

2   Pair or whole class work. Knowledge of another country often starts with traditional items or customs, and stereotypes. This exercise aims to encourage students to go beyond those stereotypes to see that Britain is a country which combines many traditional customs with more modern lifestyles. Encourage students to discuss the extent to which this is also typical of their own country.

> ### ANSWERS
>
> Photos that show traditional or stereotypic views: all of them do to some extent – the guards with their traditional uniforms, Big Ben and double decker buses, kilts and bagpipes in Scotland, music-making outside an Irish pub. Even the rainy street could be a stereotypic view of English life!
>
> Photos that show ordinary life: a policeman in uniform, travelling by bus in London, umbrellas and shopping on a rainy street. Even music making at pubs is an ordinary occurrence in many parts of Britain.

3   A quiz to draw out known information and add to it. It can be done singly, in pairs or groups. Encourage students to guess or help each other if they don't know the answers. *Note*: The flags represent (left to right) England, Scotland, Wales, Ireland.

> ### ANSWERS
>
> 1b 2a 3a 4c 5b

4   Change is very evident in Britain at the moment. In 1999, the parliaments for Scotland and Wales held their first sessions. Although their creation was based on a referendum in each country, many people fear that they will lead to further disintegration of the 'United' Kingdom. There is a perceived anomaly in the fact that Northern Ireland, Scotland and Wales each have their own assembly, but England does not. In 1999, also, radical changes were made to the second chamber of Parliament, the House of Lords, to reduce the proportion of hereditary members.

Elicit the views of students concerning these developments – do they think it is a good idea for different parts of a country to have their own assemblies and be self-governing to a certain extent? Do they believe that inherited power (as in the case of the House of Lords) is necessarily bad, or can it occasionally be useful? Encourage them to draw out as many comparisons or contrasts as they can with their own country.

5   The newspaper article reviews some of the aspects of regional differences students have been exploring, and moves on from this point to question the very notion of 'Britishness', and its relevance at a time when supra-national units (in this case the European Union) are becoming more important to people's lives. The view that 'Britishness' looks backwards to history rather than forward to the future also serves as a preparation for section C, which will take a closer look at historical events as shaping forces in a sense of identity. Encourage students to scan the text fairly quickly as a first step, to find specific answers to the four questions. The article presents an opportunity to practise gist reading.

ANSWERS

a the Scots   **b** the common religion of Protestantism, the Empire, the monarchy, and wars
c Some people (especially some Scots) do not wish to be associated with a 'United Kingdom' which they feel is in decline, while for others, 'Britishness' is connected to history, which is past, while the future of England is linked to Europe.

Elicit the response of the students to the article. Ask them to try to formulate briefly the main point that it is making about national identity. Would that point be valid in their own country?

TOWNS AND CITIES, NORTH AND SOUTH

A gist reading exercise with a puzzle element. Pairs or groups. Some of the vocabulary may be unknown, but there are clues in each of the descriptions which should allow the towns to be matched with their location on the map. Encourage students to read quickly to do the task, and not worry too much if they don't understand everything.

ANSWERS

1 Edinburgh   **2** Liverpool   **3** Brighton   **4** Durham   **5** Leeds   **6** Norwich

Again, a reading puzzle, to be done in pairs or groups.

Additional notes:

The reference in **c** is to Chaucer's *Canterbury Tales* (written between 1387 and 1392), in which a group of pilgrims tell stories on their way from London to the shrine of Thomas à Becket in Canterbury.

In recent years, Scarborough has also become well known because one of Britain's most popular dramatists, Alan Ayckbourn, has always held the first performances of his plays in this, his home town.

ANSWERS

a Belfast   **b** Caernarvon   **c** Canterbury   **d** Inverness   **e** Birmingham
f Oxford   **g** Scarborough

OPTION

Role play. An exercise which encourages students to voice their own opinions and thus personalises the geographical facts they have been working with. The first question can be a whole class discussion, followed by pair work. For a final roundup and feedback, a few volunteers could perform their role play for the class, or a class survey be done quickly, to see which were the most popular towns.

OPTIONAL FOLLOW-UP ACTIVITIES

- Quizzes. If this is useful for the class, the facts given about the towns can be revised and recycled enjoyably through quizzes. Two examples are as follows:
  a Divide the class into six. Give the class a limited time, e.g. 3–5 minutes, to study the descriptions. Books are then shut. In turn, each team is given a town. Can they recall 5 (or 6) facts to attain maximum points?
  b Divide the class into two. In a limited preparation period, each team prepares a number of questions (e.g. 10) on any of the thirteen towns described in exercises 2 and 3. In turn, they then quiz the other team.
- A written comparison (homework). Students are asked to write a short essay comparing and contrasting a British town of their choice with one in their own country. If possible, encourage research to find more facts and details about the two towns.

3 An exercise to raise awareness about the regional differences that exist in most countries. Set a time limit when students form groups to compare their ideas. Each group should then write their key ideas on the board.

4 ◖◗ Listening to authentic interviews with British students. In this first short extract, the five students interviewed simply identify themselves. Locate Bristol, Yorkshire and Somerset on the map.

ANSWERS

Anna from Bristol. Sophie from Yorkshire. Will from Bristol. Alex Turco from Somerset. Alex Ross from Bristol.

TAPESCRIPT
Unit IB, Exercise 4. An interview with five young people.
- A   My name's Anna Pearscall, and I'm from Bristol.
- S   I'm Sophie Levy, and I'm from Yorkshire.
- W   My name's Will Snell, I come from Bristol.
- AT   My name's Alex Turco, I come from Somerset.
- AR   I'm Alex Ross, I come from Bristol.

5 ◖◗ Listening, note-taking. The five students on the tape speak at their own pace, but the class can listen more than once. If your class finds listening difficult, stop the tape after each student the first time it is played, to allow note-taking. After the first listening, encourage the class to consult each other to see what details they managed to jot down. Then play the tape again through without stopping. The comparison with their own ideas can be done in pairs or as a feedback with the whole class.

TAPESCRIPT

Unit 1B, exercise 5. Five young people speak about the places they come from.

I = Interviewer   A = Anna   S = Sophie   W = Will   AT = Alex Turco   AR = Alex Ross

A I really like it, actually. There's lots of shops around … and always a lot to do. It's great. Lots of people.

S It's rather boring, really. And coming from the North … it's a lot colder than down south … and there's not much to do. And it's got a very bad reputation. Everyone's always very rude about it.

I What do you mean by a bad reputation? Why are people rude about it?

S Well, people just think the North's full of … odd people … a bit wild, really … bit backward.

I What do you think of your home town? I mean, you're still in it, aren't you?

W Yes, well I used to live in London and compared to London, Bristol is so much smaller that you can do a lot more. And … it's still big enough to be entertaining, which is a good balance.

I And you've come, Alex, you've come in from the countryside, as it were, in Somerset?

AT Well, not really the countryside. I actually live by the seaside … and we've got a beach and we get lots of tourists … There are quite a few shops but they're not really open in the winter. So in the winter it tends to be quite boring. But because I'm a boarder I'm in Bristol, there are quite a few shops, so I, there are plenty, there are plenty of activities to do.

I And you Alex, the second Alex, what do you think of your home town, which is this one, isn't it?

AR I live slightly outside Bristol so where I live is more countryside and it's rather boring but the city itself is very interesting and exciting.

6 ▶️ The prediction exercise allows any difficult words to be worked with before listening. The answer to the first two grid categories, 'affluent' and 'poor' is not straightforward. The stereotypic view is that southern Britain is more affluent than the North. National surveys show that incomes are higher in the South, but the cost of living is also much higher. On the tape, Sophie makes the sensible point that Yorkshire is a large area and has both affluent and poor people.

For the other categories, Sophie's perceptions match to a large extent the stereotypes about people in the North and South of England. This gives the opportunity of continuing to explore critically the scope and validity of stereotypes. Do stereotypes contain some measure of truth, or are they always largely false simplifications? How useful are they in thinking about groups of people? Are they a good beginning point, or are they usually harmful? Are there stereotypic notions in the key words about their own country, identified in exercise 3 in this unit?

TAPESCRIPT

Unit 1B, exercise 6. Sophie talks about the difference between the North and South in England.

I = Interviewer   S = Sophie

I And you're from Yorkshire. Ah … how would you describe … you say it has a bad reputation but perhaps you don't share that feeling. What do you think of it as a place in that sense and is it a rich area, a poor area, and what are the people like?

S … it tends to vary really, I mean Yorkshire covers a very large area, so whereas some places are very affluent you obviously get pockets of poverty as well. … The people are very, very, very, …

(laughs) … oh, got a bit carried away then! (laughs) The people are very friendly and … I don't know, I think they tend to be a bit louder than the people down south … less restrained and … perhaps less conservative in their ways.

I   Whereabouts in Yorkshire are you from?

S   … the … the East Riding of Yorkshire. On the coast, near York.

7   ⬛⬛ Here the focus shifts from regional differences to differences between a metropolis and other parts of the country. On the tape, students hear first Will from Bristol, then Sophie from Yorkshire, and finally Anna from Bristol, talking about their perceptions of life in the capital as opposed to life in a smaller town.

If students identified significant differences between urban and rural areas in their own country in exercise 1, encourage them to incorporate this comparative element into their summaries. This oral exercise can obviously lead to written homework as follow-up.

TAPESCRIPT

Unit 1B, exercise 7. The students talk about the differences between London and the rest of England.

I = Interviewer   S = Sophie   W = Will   A = Anna

I   And how do you feel about Bristol and its people?

W   I think they're very nice … They're a lot less aggressive than in London, I would say, more laid back … obviously there's variety wherever you go but … a good impression generally.

I   How long ago did you leave London?

W   Five years ago. And when … I didn't notice it at the time but when you go back, you do notice how much more aggressive and fast and stressed the life there is.

I   Have you ever been to London?

S   I've visited it and … my cousins live there. … I don't know, I think I'd prefer to live there because I mean I hope to go to university there possibly and certainly live there in the future. I'd either want to live in London or abroad. I don't think I want to live anywhere else. … That probably stems from growing up in the provinces. I think people who actually grow up in London want to get out. A lot of them go to Leeds to university, which is further north … but certainly I'd be heading for London.

I   How about you? Would you think of heading for London or is it a place you'd rather avoid?

A   For a while, I really, really wanted to live in London because of all the things to do and so many people there but I think it's really expensive. And as far as going to university there I think I'd be so poor at university anyway that I'd rather be somewhere where there wasn't quite so much expense. I think it can be, my Mum lived there for quite a while and she said that it can get really lonely there sometimes 'cause there are so many people there.

S   That's what my Dad said, 'cause he was a student there too.

C | ENGLISH HISTORY AND PLACE

1 This section starts with a look at the history of the student's own country, as a warm-up to the theme, and to set a comparative framework for the views of the British students they are going to hear next. The choice is obviously not based on right or wrong answers, but is a matter of opinion, to be negotiated within the groups. The second part of the exercise, deciding on categories, is important in that it helps students to think about the basis upon which such choices could be made, and helps them to think about what events could be important in the history of other countries as well.

2 Students work in groups. If they have previous knowledge about the history of Britain, they share and build upon it. Even if some of these events are new to them, however, they should still be able to use the categories they discussed in exercise 1 to decide which they think could have been most important in shaping the modern country.

3 ◨◨ For the first listening, stop the tape after each student's part, allowing the class to complete their answers. Then play the tape right through once again. The discussion and comparison of answers can be done as a group activity, with a spokesperson summarising the group's view at the end for the class.

ANSWERS

		Event	Reason
1	a	Roman invasion	Influence of Latin upon English
	b	Henry VIII	The continued existence of the Church of England
	c	The union of GB and Ireland	The troubles in Northern Ireland
	d	The Second World War	Shows that war is unnecessary
	e	The Beatles' albums	Started a revolution of a different type
2	a	The Roman invasion of Britain	Because all five were dates when
	b	King Alfred defeats the Danes	Britain was or nearly was invaded.
	c	The Battle of Hastings	You can't have much more of a
	d	The Battle of Waterloo	significant change than a change
	e	The Second World War	of regime.
3	a	1215 Magna Carta	The first hint of democracy
	b	Henry VIII	Gave the country a national identity
	c	The Battle of Waterloo and the Second World War	Both stopped invasion (were turning points in our history)
	d		
	e	1966: England won the World Cup	The only time we've ever done it and we're very proud!

TAPESCRIPT

Unit 1C, exercise 3. Three English students talk about their choice of events from British history.

1 ... the five I put down were the Roman invasion of Britain, ... I think 'cause I'm doing Latin I notice how much Latin has influenced English. I think that's really important. Also ... Henry the Eighth, founding the Church of England, that's part of my History syllabus. And, ... I think the break with Rome was really important. If you think about how much time has elapsed since then and the Church of England is still in existence ... the union of Great Britain and Ireland ... especially with the problems in Northern Ireland, that is so important; and I'm not sure how it can be sorted out now, it's just one of those horrible things. Also the Second World War ... I think that should be enough of a reminder to everyone that war is unnecessary. And then the Beatles' albums 'cause I think they started a revolution of a different type and any band that survives still and is so popular forty years on has got to be pretty important.

2 The five dates I chose were the Roman invasion of Britain, King Alfred defeating the Danes, the Battle of Hastings, ... the Battle of Waterloo and the Second World War, because all five were dates when Britain either was or nearly was invaded. Well I'm assuming that the Danes would have invaded if King Alfred hadn't defeated them, I'm not actually sure. But ... so and I mean for example the Second World war we almost had a Nazi regime ... and the Romans' invasion and the Battle of Hastings were obviously very important transition points and you can't really have much more of a significant change than a change of regime.

3 I think 1215 was the Magna Carta and I think that's when the sort of the first hint of sort of democracy came into the country sort of thing. There was the first sort of Parliament was first created so that's I think that's very important. Henry the Eighth founded the Church of England in about ... 1533 which was ... I think it was an important break. It gave the country some more national identity. The Battle of Waterloo and the Second World War. I think they're both sort of almost together in that they've sort of stopped a sort of greater ... probably well it was almost an invasion of ... the Battle of Waterloo I'm sure Napoleon would have come towards us if we hadn't stopped him and the Second World War Germany tried to invade us and so I think they're great turning points in history. And the fifth one I'd choose was ... 1966, I think, which, when England won the World Cup, which is the only time we've ever done it and we're very proud of it so I think it's extremely important in our history.

OPTIONAL FOLLOW-UP ACTIVITY

- If your class is interested in history, or greater knowledge would be useful to them, use the short facts given to stimulate further work. Students in pairs or groups choose one of the events and do further research, presenting their findings, for example, in the form of posters.

D LANGUAGES

The final part of this unit takes a brief look first at distinct languages other than English, then at some of the varieties of English which can be heard in the British Isles.

1 The prediction exercise serves as an introduction to some of the facts that students are going to find in the short article they are about to read.

ANSWERS

a✓ b✗ c✗ d✓ e✗ f✓

2 Encourage rapid scanning for confirmation of answers.

4 This activity, which can be done in groups or with the whole class, goes over some of the facts of the article, and elicits reactions to them. Some issues raised by the fact of having many languages in a country are thus explored.

5 The focus here is on varieties of English in different regions and social classes of the UK. This first activity introduces some of the main accents and also explains some of the terms which might be unfamiliar and cause comprehension difficulties in the article. Encourage students to guess – there are no absolutely right or wrong answers!

7 Encourage students to read through the article quickly, to check their predictions against the opinions expressed in the article.

ANSWERS

Opinions in the article: a, d (to a certain extent), e

Language notes:
'Gissa job' = 'give us a job'; 'us' for 'me' here is also part of the regional way of speaking
posh = upper-class
A standard pronunciation was sometimes known in the past as 'Oxford English' or 'the Queen's English' [or 'the King's English'].
A 'thick' accent, like a 'broad accent', means one that is very marked, very pronounced.
The 'RP brigade' = the group of people who speak standard English.
A brogue is a strongly marked regional pronunciation.

Examples of some of these accents can be heard at the following points on the tape:

RP: the three male students and Anna from Bristol (Unit 1B, ex 4, 5, 7; Unit 1C, ex 3; Unit 5B, ex 8; Unit 6A, ex 3; Unit 8A, ex 3, 7, 8; Unit 10B, ex 2.1, ex 5); Wendy and Richard (Unit 3A, ex 3; Unit 9C ex 2–5); Tim Fywell (Unit 6C, ex 6)

Scottish (Edinburgh): Scottish students (Unit 4C, ex 3; Unit 5B, ex 3; Unit 6A, ex 4; Unit 10B, ex 2, 5; Unit 10D, ex 2, 3)

Indian: Mr and Mrs Gupta (Unit 2B, ex 2)

West Indian: poems (Unit 2A, ex 5)

'Mellow provincial brogues': Andrew (Unit 3A, ex 3 – Derbyshire); Sophie (Unit 1B, ex 6, 7; Unit 5B, ex 8; Unit 8A, ex 3, 7, 8; Unit 10B, ex 2.1, ex 5 – Yorkshire); Roger McGough (Unit 7D, ex 2, 3 – Liverpool)

As a follow-up to reading the article, students should be encouraged to say whether or not they agree with it, and give reasons. One of the important aspects of 'cultural studies' is the emphasis on critical reading of texts. Here, students should realise that, unlike the short article they read in exercise 2, which was largely factual, this one puts forward opinions which can be challenged or with which readers can disagree. British readers of the article usually have strong reactions to it: some do feel that it is unacceptable because it stereotypes people on the basis of their accent; others are convinced that although the situation outlined in the article may have existed in the past, it no longer does in the present. Many disagree – some violently – with the individual opinions expressed, for example that women with RP voices are thought to be more confident, adventurous, etc. Encourage students to voice their own opinions and discuss reasons for them.

FOLLOW-UP PROJECT

The following project provides an opportunity for doing further work on areas of this unit which may have particularly interested students. It is usually more enjoyably done as pair or group work.

This unit has focused upon differences between various groups of people within one country. These differences can be regional, for example those between North and South. They can emerge through language (accent, dialects), the aspect particularly examined here, or through clothing, customs, food, the temperament of the people, the climate, class, education or social status.

Students choose one aspect that they find interesting. They do research to find out more about differences within Britain, to compare them with the situation in their own country. Materials that can be used include newspapers, magazines, reference books, encyclopaedias, tourist brochures, etc. If possible, students can interview people who come from different parts of the country, travel agents, etc.

The results and findings of the project can be presented in one of the following ways:
– Oral presentation
– Poster
– Illustrated essay
– Video

CULTURAL DIVERSITY

- To provide a multilateral view of Britain's ethnically mixed society
- To help students identify some of the feelings and experiences associated with living in a foreign country
- To sketch out the history of immigration to Britain since World War II
- To consider the advantages and disadvantages of a multicultural society
- To look at questions of cultural conflict both in Britain and in their own society

GENERAL REMARKS

As well as the regional and national differences that we examined in Unit 1, there are important ethnic and cultural diversities in the population of Britain which are the subject of this unit. Migration to the British Isles is at least 6,000 years old, but it has become an 'issue' in the last 50 years with the arrival (encouraged by the Government) of significant numbers of non-white immigrants, mainly from India and the Caribbean. The colour of people's skin is, of course, an unacceptable basis for discrimination, but this has played a part in the life of Britain which, however regrettable, has to be acknowledged. Gradually, and not always very smoothly, integration, acceptance, racial harmony and equality are being established – by law and by a deep, slow change in people's attitudes. The process has greatly enriched the life of Britain. In our food, music, literature, sport, theatre, television and many other areas of our daily lives, we live in a context of far greater ethnic and global awareness than ever before. And even if this can be partly explained by the information revolution, increased world travel, etc., an immense amount of goodwill and understanding has been achieved in quiet, invisible ways by ordinary people of all ethnic backgrounds: there is a strong sense of this in the interview with the Indian family in part B.

An important element in this unit is exposure to 'non standard English', as spoken in various forms both outside and inside the British Isles. Teachers sometimes feel threatened by this, fearing that all their hard work in teaching the correct spellings and grammatical forms will be lost, as students read poems written, for example, in a phonetic version of Caribbean speech, or listen to interviewees speaking Indian English. We take the view that all these Englishes are authentic and legitimate (like the regional Englishes of Britain), and should be enjoyed for the new life and vibrancy they have brought to the language and literature of Britain. Students' ability to use standard English need not be threatened by awareness of these other varieties; in fact their ability may well be enhanced by exercises drawing attention to grammatical and lexical differences – or, perhaps even more importantly, through the pleasures of experiencing those varieties directly for themselves.

A | A NEW COUNTRY

The idea here is to look at the question of 'immigration' from the migrant's point of view. By placing themselves in the position of 'guests' rather than 'hosts' (or 'them' rather than 'us'), students should gain a refreshing new perspective on the political and human issues involved.

1 We have found this exercise most effective as a form of 'guided fantasy'. The students sit quietly, with no books open, no distractions, only a pen and a sheet of paper in front of them. The teacher gives simple, calm instructions, creating an atmosphere in which the mind feels free to travel at its own speed, to its own imagined place. The teacher can choose whether to ask students to write the poem during the guided fantasy or after it. It is helpful to write the cues on a board or OHP after saying them ('I look out of the window', etc.). There is of course no 'right' or 'wrong' fantasy. The essential thing is for each student to take part in the imaginative experience and have something of their own written down at the end of it. Some may feel shy about calling their writing a 'poem', but most will be pleasantly surprised at how vivid their own and others' poems turn out to be.

3 For this exercise, pairs from the last exercise stay together. If you have, for example, 16 pairs in the class, 8 pairs should read *Back Home* and the other 8 *Wherever I Hang*. It is important at this stage to keep the two groups separate, and working only on the poem they have been assigned. (Language notes for these poems are on pages 22 and 23.)

> **ANSWER**
>
> The two writers come from the Caribbean.

5   There is an opportunity here for connections with other aspects of British culture, including the classic British topic of conversation, the weather. (See Unit 9B. This is not, perhaps, as trivial as it may seem. Grace Nichols connects weather, mood and social customs in many subtle ways.)

> **ANSWERS**
>
> Possible difficulties in England
> *Wherever I Hang:* the weather – misty greyness, the cold and snow; the houses – the 'unreal' walls; the crowds – pouring from the underground; the formality of personal relations – give clear warnings before visiting, wait in queues.
> *Back Home:* the cold – no hot sun, lack of fresh fruit growing in garden, the cold sea.
>
> What might be liked
> *Wherever I Hang:* possibly a better standard of living (no rats in the floorboard); the novelty of being in a big city (sending home photos of herself with pigeons in Trafalgar Square); gradually accepting English ways.
> *Back Home:* very little or no positive feelings about the new country.

6 This exercise involves prediction. Students should be encouraged to think about the questions and answer them from their existing knowledge, or by intelligent guesswork, or through discussion, before turning the page.

B   NEW CITIZENS OF BRITAIN

1 Encourage students to read through the article quickly to check their predictions or guesses.

ANSWERS

> **a** The largest numbers came from countries that were once part of the British Empire in Africa, Asia and the Caribbean. There were also significant numbers of immigrants from China, the Middle East and Southern Europe (especially Italy, Greece, Spain).
>
> **b** Better economic prospects is the main reason given, but other possible answers include encouragement by the British Government, educational opportunities and family connections.
>
> **c** The answer to this is not explicitly stated, but the historical record suggests an initial mixture of hostility and condescension, tempered with some genuine friendliness and attempts to help (these contradictory attitudes are also expressed in the various Acts of Parliament mentioned). The hostility seems generally to have decreased with time. The various Immigration Acts limiting numbers of immigrants indicate that official attempts have been made to stop people coming to Britain.
>
> **d** Racial discrimination in jobs and housing (now illegal, although some studies of employment indicate that this is still a problem). Other problems (not mentioned here) include cultural conflicts over education, clothing, religion, customs and beliefs, racist attitudes, etc.
>
> **e** 6%.

2 Listening, note-taking. This interview presents an Indian family's experiences of living in Britain.

ANSWERS

> *Part A*
>
> **1** The number of cars, the rows of houses (terraced housing), how much daylight there still is at ten o'clock at night
>
> **2** The weather, friends, open-air evening activities
>
> **3** She teaches people English as a second language.
>
> *Part B*
>
> **1** Being badly treated when he was promoted and became a quality inspector; people making silly remarks about Indians being backward, people not wishing to work under him or resenting being told what to do by him.

2 Helping those who could not read to fill in their tax forms; helping them with their language difficulties, when they met doctors, etc.; keeping them in touch with Indian culture through celebrations, cinema, social clubs, entertainment; helping them to write to their families and sort out their problems.

Part C

I He can't say whether he's British or Indian. He is both.

2 His friends go out every weekend, to pubs, get drunk. Indians stay with their families more.

3 When he worked for a large supermarket (Sainsbury's) he was the one to be given menial jobs like collecting the trolleys from the car parks; people driving past used to shout things at him, but this has not happened for the last 4 or 5 years.

TAPESCRIPT
Unit 2B, exercise 2. An interview with the Gupta family.

Part A. Mrs Gupta, the mother.
I = Interviewer   M = Mother

I What image of Britain did you have in your mind before you left India?

M Well, I thought it have … it will be very big houses, nice bungalow and all this stuff, but when I came to England, when I get off from the airport, I was amazed by cars, it was lots of, lots of cars, but when I came to my house it wasn't like I was expecting, it's like a street, all row for houses, which I wasn't expecting, I was expecting big houses, and all these things, but it was totally different, it was bit disappointed, and one thing I was amazed when I got off from the plane, it was ten o'clock at night and it was still quite light, day time, and I was thinking it should be night time here, why it's so light up here? And well, I didn't know days are that longer here, and that was the new thing for me when I came over here.

I Do you enjoy living in Britain?

M Yes I do, yes, yes. But still I can't forget the back, yes.

I When you say you can't – you can't forget what?

M I'm enjoying at the moment, yes, it is nice to live here with the family and because most of our family is here, from my mum's side as well, and Paul's side as well. But sometimes when you remember back in India you want to go back, yes.

I What do you miss?

M It's mostly the weather. Because weather is, up there weather is nice, it's a proper season, you know. We do have rainy season as well, winter, a proper winter as well, and summer as well, so it's a bit different than here, and the weather was fantastic up there.

I What else do you miss apart from the weather?

M Friends! And in the evening atmosphere.

I Tell me about that a bit.

M Well, up here it's … all you do, it's mostly indoors. But over there it's open air, most of the things, you can go for a walk in the evening, beautiful gardens and all this stuff. And up here even it's nice gardens and things, but weather spoils it.

I   I know you're involved in an English teaching project in Oxford and I'd like you to tell me something about that now. What sort of people do you teach?

M   … Well I mostly teach people whose language is, English is a second language. Well, mostly people are from Pakistan, Bangladesh and India, and some of them have got Chinese students as well, and Korean, and sometimes … one girl we got from Russia as well. So I teach most of them, yeah, if their English, if they need in English, so I teach them as well.

Part B. Mr Gupta, the father.

I = *Interviewer*   F = *Father*

I   What work did you go into after you finished studying?

F   I work for Rover Group now and have been working there for twenty-four years, so it's OK.

I   What do you do at Rover?

F   I work for Quality Department, I'm a quality inspector there … you know I did find it very difficult in the beginning. When become a quality inspector people were not very happy at all, they treated me really bad in those days I suppose because they didn't like to work under me at all sort of you know, they were making some silly remarks and it was difficult in the beginning but gradually it come all right sort of, yes, that's OK.

I   So you found it difficult because you were senior to …

F   Exactly.

I   … to white English people, who felt …

F   That's right, yes, because there's some people see has been working there for a long time, say, twenty years, or thirty years, and if you will tell them something and they wouldn't like it at all. And they were making some silly remarks that – oh what do you know about the cars, in India they were building bullock carts, this and that, so it was really very, very bad anyway – behaviour anyway – and … but I tolerate all right … Yes.

I   Were there other Indians at work?

F   Not many people were working in those days in the Rover Group, no, no, only few.

I   Has that changed now?

F   Oh yes yes yes, it is changed quite a lot now anyway. From time to times the things have improved a lot now, and the behaviours among the foreigners and all that is marvellous now, no problem at all. Excellent. Yes.

I   Now I know that when you came home from work you used to organise social evenings. Can you tell me something about that?

F   Because in the beginning there were not many Indian peoples, and they didn't have their family here. And they were missing their family, and a lot of people come from the village, and some people were illiterate, and they had a language problem, and they didn't know much about how to fill their Inland Revenue form, DHSS, or whenever they go to doctors, what to say and all that, and they were missing their cultures, they were missing their socials, life, and what we tried to arrange that … in '65 we establish here the Indian Associations, and with that we form societies, and then we used to celebrate our Indian festival, festival, and we used to celebrate our Independence Day, and then we start running the cinema as well, Asian cinema, so people can come and watch it, and it was good for their social and cultural life and entertainment, and it was good. And so we used to go to the people's different houses and if they got any problem, or some time if they want to write a letter to … to back their own families, and I used to help them out, and you know if they got any problems try to sort out; and meet them, to communicate anyway. It was marvellous, yes. Spent a lot of time! – with them … Good. So they don't feel any neglect or anything like that at all, they don't have much problem, and it was good, yes.

Language notes:

'Rover Group' = a car manufacturer

'Inland Revenue' = Government tax office

'DHSS' = Government Department of Health and Social Security

Part C. The son.

I = Interviewer   S = Son

I   Do you feel Indian or British?

S   I think I feel a bit … like I can't say like one or the other, 'cause I've been brought up here in England and I've got most of the British culture and everything, but I still have the Indian background in me, so I don't really think I can say I'm British or Indian.

I   Do you feel that there are parts of you which are Indian and parts of you which are British?

S   Yeah, yeah, definitely.

I   Can you tell me a bit more about what those parts are?

S   Well, things like my friends get up to and stuff like they, like say they go out on the weekends and stuff, like every weekend, I don't think it's in the Indian culture, like to go out and leave like your family on the weekends and stuff, so I think the Indian culture is more like family like orientated rather than like spending, going out with your friends more.

I   So what do your friends go and do? What is it that they're going out and doing which you … which is typically British?

S   Going out to the pubs, getting drunk, and …

I   This is something that a young person in India just wouldn't do, is that right?

S   I don't think so, no.

I   What about racism? Have you ever had any problems with that?

S   There are some things that you can like, point to racisms, but not … not in a serious manner. Like, I worked for Sainsbury's, and what they … my position was like, on checkouts, and what they used to do was take me off checkouts and take me outside and do … collect all the trolleys from the car parks. And now I used to do that every week, and … there were a lot of other boys who could have gone out and done the same thing, but they seem to have always picked on me – which you can't really say is racism or it's not, but it's one of those things that you can point to racism, but then again it might not have been.

I   That's a very mild form of racism, isn't it? I mean I was thinking of the … there have been some much more vicious things that have gone on. Have you ever suffered being called unpleasant names, or anything like that?

S   Well you do get the occasional like some, someone like driving past will shout out and say something sometimes, but that used to happen, but I haven't like, nothing like that has happened to me within like, oh, about four or five years, so no, no.

3 *Language notes:*

'compound' = garden

'jammed against each other' = crowded uncomfortably together

'Formica-topped table' = a table with a surface made of 'Formica'. Formica is a hard, laminated material which became popular in the 1950s for kitchen furniture. Having a Formica table between the settee and the bed is a clear sign of very cramped, utilitarian accommodation.

ANSWERS

The obvious similarity is the surprise at English terraced housing ('long solid blocks, with doors opening into the street'). Things mentioned by the Indian mother that are not in this extract: weather, long light evenings, indoor life.

4 Like the heroine of her novel, Buchi Emecheta was born and educated in Nigeria. She moved to England in 1962, and has since written eleven novels, four children's books and an autobiography as well as radio and TV plays. One of the most remarkable aspects of her writing is her ability to arouse sympathy for her characters while also playing ironically with stereotypes. Adah and Francis expect England to be a wealthy and advanced society – yet the housing is squalid, cramped and degrading, far inferior to the spacious homes they have left behind in Nigeria. Her husband Francis, who has come to London ahead of his family, already accepts that Africans can get nothing better. As well as the more obvious points mentioned in the Answers below, there are several subtle details in the passage which students may pick up – the lack of individuality in the houses, their similarity to churches or monasteries (implying a strict, spartan existence), and the harsh economic choices suggested by the fact that Francis could only buy a settee with money intended for a coat.

ANSWERS

Conditions in England	Conditions in Nigeria
joined to other houses	completely detached, yards on both sides
long solid blocks	compound at back, verandas in front
doors opening into street	
windows arranged in straight rows	(more space) 'can afford to waste land'
looked like a tunnel – it was a hall	spacious verandas
a room – or half room	
the space … just enough for a table	
the toilet outside, four flights down	
no bath, no kitchen	
a nasty pill	

C 'THAT'S MY HOME'

Language notes for 'Wherever I Hang':

'me people', 'de sun', etc.: 'me' is a phonetic spelling of *my* in colloquial Caribbean speech, as is 'de' for *the*, and 'belaang' for *belong*. Other (grammatical) characteristics are: the verb 'to be' either as a main verb or as an auxiliary verb is often missing, and past participles are phonetically written without final *-ed* ('this place call England'). This suits the compression of poetic language very well, and the effect is often both attractive and memorable.

'Lord Nelson': a naval hero (1758–1805) whose early career included service in the West Indies. He is one of the key figures in British military and imperial history, and his statue is placed on an immensely high column in Trafalgar Square in London.

'too high to lie': this implies that he is too great a hero to tell lies – an ironic thought.

'warding off de cold' = trying to keep the cold away, to keep warm

'calypso': traditional form of Caribbean song. Here it stands for a whole way of living.

'back-home side' = the life back home

'knickers' (colloquial) = a woman's underwear. There is a deliberate and abrupt change of tone here, suggesting that the reality of life is ultimately domestic and intimate.

1
2
These are activities which the teacher can shape or extend as they choose. Essentially, they provide an opportunity for students to observe and draw conclusions. They could lead to a discussion, a debate, an essay, or, in conjunction with exercise 2 on page 20, a project of a more creative kind: a journalistic investigation, a drama, or even a video presentation.

For suggestions on organising a debate, see Teacher's Notes for Unit 3 Part A, exercise 7 on page 27.

Language notes:

4 'remanded in custody' = imprisoned until they are tried in a court of justice

5 'the extended family' = the wider family of aunts, uncles, cousins, grandparents, all in close contact with each other. The phrase is often used in contrast to 'the nuclear family', which means only parents and children living together.

6 'to foster a benign cycle of upward mobility': this is a typical journalistic phrase containing a mixed metaphor. To 'foster' is literally to act as parent to another person's child; here it means to encourage and allow. A 'benign cycle' is a medical term for a healing process in which one improvement leads to another. 'Upward mobility' means moving upwards in society. So the whole phrase means something like 'to help them to advance socially'.

7 'damned if you're going to' (strong language) = angrily determined not to; 'precepts' = rules of behaviour; 'collective consciousness' = the ideas and beliefs of a whole community.

ANSWERS

Positive aspects: more prosperous Asians (300 millionaires); immaculate condition of Italian houses; retaining Italian customs, e.g. making wine, growing vegetables, colourful, well maintained paintwork, early morning delivery of Italian bread; the strength that comes from their culture, religion, family; Western educational and career opportunities; some progress in race relations in recent years; a growing, articulate, black middle class; second generation Britons are more confident than their parents and have upward mobility.

Negative aspects: unemployment (a coloured person has to be twice as good as an English person to get a job – 15% compared to 8% for white people); blacks are more likely to be arrested, charged, kept in custody, imprisoned; colour awareness is always present.

D | CULTURAL CONFLICT

1 There are no readymade solutions to these problems, although in both cases quoted here the authorities eventually yielded. Thinking of arguments both for and against may be difficult for students, and some imagination will be required. Why should Bedford Town Council insist on 'placing' rather than 'growing' flowers on graves? Or object to little fences? Presumably because of an aesthetic convention, a tradition, a wish to respect the British families whose dead are buried in the cemetery. The Islamic school poses trickier questions, such as whether a government should help to educate children in a religious philosophy that imposes rules and codes which the government does not recognise. (Note that such schools were allowed to exist as private institutions, but the difficulty arose with the request for state aid.) In non-Islamic countries it may help to provide some information about Islam as background material to this exercise.

There is a photograph of a class in the Islamia School on page 21.

3 It's a good idea to have some examples of your own for this exercise, perhaps in the form of newspaper cuttings. Students may not have the required knowledge of current affairs and recent history to provide their own.

'A TV documentary' may seem rather ambitious or time-consuming, but a live presentation in the form of a TV documentary works just as well, is quicker to prepare, and is usually more enjoyable to watch.

Language notes for 'Back Home':
Like *Wherever I Hang* this poem uses some elements of Caribbean English. It's worth noticing the presence of the emphatic 'does' with several verbs here, while in other places the verb is simply dropped ('I not back home'). The effect is to linger on the verbs with 'does' (as the mind lingers on pleasant memories), and to reduce some other phrases to the barest minimum (as the mind tries to pass quickly over painful things). With 'the sea does chill your feet' at the end there is an exception to this, which perhaps suggests a mind facing up to comfortless reality in an explicit way.

SPORT

- To give students a sense of the importance of sport to people in Britain today
- To provide a historical context for today's attitudes to sport
- To elicit students' opinions and invite comparisons with their own attitudes and ideas
- To give an idea of the continuing debate on the philosophy of sport, particularly over questions of its moral value and the advantages and disadvantages of professionalism

GENERAL REMARKS

British attitudes to sport are complex and fascinating. They vary from passionate rejection to an almost religious belief in the value of sport as a means of personal, social, moral, educational or business development. Even among those who love sport, there is a division between those who admire the ideal of 'sportsmanship' (playing with skill, courtesy and respect for the rules) and those who believe only in winning.

The historical contribution of Britain to the codification and dissemination of many popular sports is, of course, enormous. Sport has long been an essential part of British education, and is perhaps second only to the weather as a topic of conversation.

We have looked at sport from both the spectator's and participator's point of view, and invited comparison between the two. Opportunities are offered for cross-cultural comparison, and for thought about the role of sport in the students' own lives.

A SPORTS THROUGH THE AGES

1 A vocabulary exercise and mental warm-up, which will help to prepare students for the text in exercise 5; also an opportunity to check pronunciation, extend vocabulary and clear out a few 'false friends' which exist in a number of languages where English words are used with non-English meanings.

2 An extension of exercise 1, which may elicit more specific names of sports and recycle any new ones.

3 ▱▱ In this exercise, students have to deduce the names of sports from clues given by the four speakers on the tape. The sports are not named. If your class finds this listening difficult, play each speaker separately, and ask students to write down *any* important words they recognise; this should lead them to the answer. The pictures at the top of the page may also help, although Richard's favourite sport is rowing rather than sailing.

ANSWERS

Name	Clues	Sport
Jacqui	country walk + purpose, fairway, club, hit into the trees, swing, drive, 150 yards, par four, green, six feet from the pin	golf
Andrew	the ball hitting the middle of the racquet, Bjorn Borg, Tim Henman	tennis
Richard	water, a boat on the Thames, go up and down the river quietly and take exercise	rowing
Wendy	space, time to look around and appreciate what's going on in the countryside, uphill, climb a mountain	walking

TAPESCRIPT

Unit 3A, exercise 3. Four people talk about their favourite sports.

J = Jacqui   A = Andrew   R = Richard   W = Wendy

J You know, we're stood here, on a hill, with trees and the countryside and rabbits watching, you know, and ponds and wildlife basically, and we think, well, we wouldn't have done this for a walk, and we think, you know, it's just such a wonderful way to spend time. It's, it's … I mean I do go for country walks as well, but no, it gives a sort of purpose, it's a purpose, it's a reason for being out there … I can hit the ball straight down the fairway at the full capacity, I can suddenly time the ball so sweet that it will sing off my club and go straight down the middle of the fairway, and I stand there like a king, you know. And yet the next time I'll hit it into the trees … Just stand there, get your shape of your body right, address the ball, draw your swing back carefully and let fly. And I hit three beautiful drives, onto the … it was a par four and I was onto the green in three, and the third shot, from about a hundred and fifty yards back, landing six feet from the pin – I could have cried.

A I like it because I don't have to run as much as I used to; I like the experience of the good … I like the experience of a good shot … The sensation of the ball hitting the middle of the racquet and going where you want it to go is very satisfying. So that, I think, is very pleasing … And like no other activity, you can imagine that although you might be a decrepit forty-one year-old bashing a ball about, for a moment whilst you're waiting to receive that ball from your daughter, you can be momentarily Bjorn Borg or Tim Henman or whoever it might be for that split second because you're doing exactly what they do, but in fact you're playing in the local municipal park …

R   I like most things to do with water – either falling in the water, or swimming in the water, or riding on the water, or sailing. I like the smell of the river banks and the smell of the sea, and the sort of things you can do associated with water … We have a share via a club in a boat on the Thames and that's available for any two people who can get the boat in the water, so it's only ten minutes from my house and we can go on the evenings of the summer when it's particularly nice to go up and down the river quietly and take exercise and be in wonderful surroundings.

W   Well the first thing is that you have space, you have fresh air, and you have time to think, you have time to look around you, you have time to appreciate what's going on in the countryside, and very often you have time to solve the problems that can't be solved in the week … The most important thing is not to spend very much time in the car getting there, but to be outside as much as possible. If it's a weekend, then I would prefer to go somewhere where there is more uphill, and so the nearest to where I live would be the Welsh border, where it's quite possible to climb a mountain, which is more exciting.

4 This can be done in pairs or small groups. Students with a good knowledge of history may know some of the answers, but the aim here is to stimulate curiosity and thought rather than to test prior knowledge.

5 Reading for specific information. Encourage students to find what they are looking for quickly and efficiently, but insist on accurate quotation to support their views. Question (a) has several answers from different parts of the text.

ANSWERS

a   Various differences are mentioned:
   Paragraph 1: prohibition of sports 'because rulers feared they might divert men from remaining in a state of readiness for war'. Paragraphs 3 and 5: amateurism (5th to 16th centuries; 1896 Olympics). Paragraph 7: increasing participation of women.

b   There were sports professionals in Classical times (boxers, wrestlers, jockeys, athletes and chariot drivers are mentioned in paragraph 3), and in 18th and 19th century Britain (boxing, cricket, football, rugby, golf).

c   The 19th century.

d   Football, rugby, badminton, croquet, lawn tennis, cricket, squash, snooker and table tennis. (They are listed in paragraph 2.)

e   No. See the answer to a, paragraph 1, above.

f   Victorian fashions (heavy, restrictive clothing), and men's belief that sport was 'unbecoming for women'.

---

7 The aim of this activity is to help students to think about their own attitudes to sport, so that they can make more sensitive and informed judgements on those of others.

ORGANISING A MINI-DEBATE

1 Choosing sides.
  - For larger classes: divide into an even number of groups – half of them prepare arguments supporting one of the themes, the others prepare arguments against. Smaller classes can be simply divided into two.

2 Preparing the debate.
  - Encourage brainstorming within groups as a first step to gathering all possible ideas. One person makes notes and records the suggestions made.
  - In any debate, the process of persuading people involves pointing out why the opposite ideas are not correct or useful. In preparing, students should therefore think not only of arguments for their side of the theme: equally important is the process of imagining what arguments could be made against their ideas, and thinking of ways of countering them – 'rebutting' or 'rebuttal' are terms for this which are often used in debates.
  - If there is time, or as homework, groups can do more research into the arguments that they wish to use. For example, they could consult books or newspapers in the library. Quotes from experts or simply from written sources can be used to support their own views, or to counter the views of the opposing side.
  - Remind students that they are trying to convince others – structuring a clear argument, using wit or humour, supporting with facts/statistics – all these are likely to be useful persuasive strategies.

3 Holding the debate.
  - An informal mini-debate: two groups line up on each side of the classroom. Students speak in turn – first a person from the 'pro' side (supporting the theme) then one from the 'against' side. They continue until one side runs out of arguments and cannot continue. The other group thus emerges as the 'winners'.
  - In larger classes, one group can line up against another. Each person has the opportunity to speak once. Other groups listen, and then discuss which side was most persuasive and why. The other groups then present their own mini-debate on another topic.
  - In classes where there is more time, and where students are likely to enjoy this kind of activity, a more formal type of debate can be organised. In this format, there is someone presiding, who calls upon each speaker and makes sure that they don't go over their time allocation (say two to five minutes each). The speakers present their arguments in turn. There is then an opportunity for each team to rebut the opposing side's ideas. In some types of debate, the floor is then opened to listeners, who can make their own points about the issues discussed. There is then a vote (either a pre-selected 'jury' of listeners, or a vote amongst all the listeners) to decide which side has been most persuasive.

---

8 The history of sport is full of surprises, and reflects the evolution of society in many interesting ways. Decide whether you prefer students to adopt a national or international approach, and encourage them to look at the social and cultural history of a particular sport rather than the bare facts of the sporting record: that is, rather than long lists of gold medallists, an account of the general development of the sport – its beginnings, early competitions, its institutions and some key personalities.

When making posters, students should try to think of images as well as words, and be as inventive as possible in design. Pictures should complement the text and convey useful information. Students can add photographs, cuttings from magazines, photocopied or scanned material from books, diagrams, etc.

B | THE SPORTING CALENDAR

1 This passage (or part of it) can simply be read by the students, or used as a dictation, or adapted to make a gap-filling exercise.

2 This exercise focuses on some useful words and expressions which students can use in the rest of the unit.

> **ANSWERS**
>
> **a** venue   **b** spectators   **c** exclusive   **d** beyond the reach of   **e** there is great demand

3 The first cross-cultural element in the unit, as well as a preparation for exercise 4. Some connections with the history of sport may also come up here. Encourage students to talk about events they have seen live as well as on TV.

4 Pictures as well as texts can be used for information in this activity. You can get oral feedback from this exercise by asking those with Role Cards 1 and 3 to report on their findings. Encourage them to make notes for this purpose. An alternative written method is offered in exercise 5.

5 Information which should be included in the sporting calendar:

January–March: Five Nations Championship (rugby): London, Edinburgh, Cardiff, Dublin, Paris.
Last Saturday in March: Oxford & Cambridge Boat Race: River Thames in London.
March: The Grand National: Aintree (Liverpool).
May: FA Cup Final: Wembley. Also Scottish Cup Final: Hampden Park.
June–August: Test Matches (cricket): various grounds, including Lord's.
June: Royal Ascot: Ascot Heath.
June (first Saturday): The Derby: Epsom Downs.
End of June; All-England Championships (tennis), also known as Wimbledon: Wimbledon (south London).
July: Henley Royal Regatta: Henley-on-Thames.

C | LIKES AND DISLIKES

1 Students will probably guess according to their own preferences. This is fine.

Language notes:
'netball': similar to basketball, played by teams of 7 girls.
'aerobics' = a strenuous form of keep-fit exercise made popular by the actress Jane Fonda.
'rounders' = a simple form of baseball, often played in British primary schools.
'ten-pin bowling' (often known simply as 'bowling'): an indoor sport where a large ball is rolled down an alley at a set of ten skittles or pins.

2 You will need to find out what the top five sports are in your country; such information is usually available from a central sporting organisation or government department. Students can investigate this for homework or guess the answer and check it with you. Differences between countries can be explained in various ways, including climate, historical tradition, government policy, etc.

3/4 An introduction to the question of the moral value of sport, as well as a vocabulary-building exercise.

ANSWERS

(These are suggestions. Others are possible, of course.)

Words	Synonyms	Antonyms
honourable	decent, honest, fair	dishonourable
boring	dull	exciting, lively
generous	kind, unselfish	mean, petty, selfish
useless	futile, pointless	useful, productive, fruitful
keen	very interested, committed	indifferent, uninterested
unselfish	kind, considerate, altruistic	selfish, egotistical
free	unrestricted	restricted, constrained
moral	ethical, good	immoral, unethical
decent	considerate, fair, equitable, honourable	inconsiderate, unfair, dishonourable
sordid	(physically) foul, dirty	clean
	(morally) mean	unselfish, noble
happy	contented, glad	unhappy, miserable, sad
boastful	conceited and loud	modest
fair play	justice, equity	injustice, cheating
violence	excessive force, aggression	peacefulness, gentleness
pleasure	happiness, joy, a good feeling	pain, suffering
hatred	extreme dislike, loathing	love
terror	extreme fear	confidence
jealousy	envy, possessiveness, rancour	generosity, ability to share

5 This is an example of how language reflects habits of mind and social tradition. The figurative expressions mentioned here are common in English, together with others such as 'below the belt' (which comes from boxing, and refers to illegal or unkind behaviour). Students should try to think of figurative rather than literal expressions, and you may need to help them with some examples of your own. If there is no connection in the students' language between sport and ethics, this is of course an interesting point of contrast with English, and it may well be interesting to reflect on what field of activity or lexis is used for such figurative expressions: is it agriculture, food, trade, love, war …?

6 **ANSWERS**

Suggested positions:

```
                              H | C                        (A)
                                | pleasure

        D                     G                           F, I
        _____
        negative                                  positive
        moral value                               moral value

                                                            E

                              B | suffering
```

7 A personalising activity designed to re-process ideas and vocabulary used in this unit. It is important that students should give consideration to views opposite to their own, even if they choose to write a defence of their views rather than a dialogue.

D **FOOTBALL: FANS AND PLAYERS**

1 Another example of how social and sporting history interact: students could be asked to think about the broader developments in society suggested by these changes, as well as the more specific comparisons between football in their country and in Britain.

Language notes:
'terraces' = sloping areas of concrete where spectators stand to watch a football match.

2 A personalising activity. Sporting events recalled can be professional or amateur.

3 This should be done individually, followed perhaps by comparing with a partner or in small groups. The aim is to prepare and motivate students for the following exercise.

4 *Language notes:*
Mr Wright
'stick' (slang) = criticism
'company car' = a car offered by a company to an employee

'BUPA' = private health insurance

'turn it down' = refuse it

'mugs' (slang) = fools

Fever Pitch

'the likes of us' = people like us

'Wembley' = the national football stadium of England

'Princess Diana': there is usually a member of the royal family at major sporting events. *Fever Pitch* was written before the death of Princess Diana in 1997.

'how football is consumed': 'consumed' here means appreciated, understood, felt by the people who watch it.

'poles/handles': the image is from table football, where the miniature players are mounted on metal poles and manoeuvred with handles.

'shoddily' = badly

'the Littlewoods Cup' = a national football competition.

ANSWERS

Criticism of fans (Ian Wright):

'Fans want it all their way every time'

'they cannot respect that a player wants to better himself'

'It's crazy: none of the values of real life matter where fans are concerned'

'sometimes it's a hell of a job trying to make them see sense'

Defence of fans:

'I love the passion and enthusiasm and love that fans bring to the game' (Ian Wright)

'I worked every bit as hard for it as they did. The only difference between me and them is that I have put in more hours, more years, more decades than them, and so had a better understanding of the afternoon, a sweeter appreciation of why the sun still shines when I remember it.' (Nick Hornby)

Criticism of players:

There is none directly expressed in either passage, but Ian Wright is replying to the accusation of treachery – or lack of loyalty to a club – and Nick Hornby implies something similar when he says that 'the players are merely our representatives', and that fans 'put in more hours, more years, more decades than them'.

Defence of players (Ian Wright):

'a player wants to better himself in his playing standards and financially'

'why should a footballer be any different?'

5 ## ANSWER

The first says more about money, the second more about feelings.

UNIT

4   FOOD

AIMS

- To provide an awareness of the traditional foods of Britain
- To suggest the changing attitudes to food in Britain today
- To connect food with other aspects of life, notably work, health, traditions of hospitality and the diversity of cultures
- To help students think about food and cultural identity

GENERAL REMARKS

Eating habits in Britain today are varied and eclectic. While large sections of the community eat and drink very much as they have for the past 50 or 100 years, others have changed their diet radically, influenced by a series of important changes. These include a spectacular increase in the number of food programmes on TV, a relentless rise in the power and profits of supermarkets, a growing gastronomic awareness and sophistication and the widespread availability of foods and spices from all over the world. There is also growing public concern over health and food safety – particularly in the light of 'mad cow disease', genetically modified crops, and a general suspicion that scientists do not always know (or tell us) what is best for us, particularly if they work for large international food companies.

Many such changes are also taking place in other countries, although few perhaps have seen such an immense rise in the level of popular interest, from insularity and indifference to fascination and a cosmopolitan appetite for experiment.

In this unit, we have sought to connect the topic of food with deeper social changes, without becoming over-solemn. It is certainly possible to 'kill' even such a vital and enjoyable theme as food by burying it in statistics and analysis. We hope students will feel at ease with the subject, and enjoy speculating on its social connections and implications without fear of making mistakes. Those who have visited Britain (including teachers) will certainly have plenty to write, think and talk about.

A   THE TRADITIONAL FOODS OF BRITAIN

1 This is a simple identification exercise in which the names of the foods themselves provide clues. If students do not know the answers, you could ask them to say the names of the dishes aloud. Do they *sound* English? There is one exception to this rule on the menu: 'sweet and sour pork' is an English name for a Chinese dish.

ANSWERS

Underlined dishes are British. Other nationalities are given in brackets.

Starters

<u>Prawn cocktail</u>

Melon with Parma ham (*Italian*)

<u>Smoked salmon</u>

Vegetable samosas (*Indian*)

<u>Kipper pâté with toast</u>

Taramasalata (*Greek*)

<u>Oxtail soup</u>

Main courses

Seafood

<u>Deep fried cod or haddock and chips</u>

<u>Herrings in oatmeal with mustard sauce</u>

Paella (*Spanish*)

<u>Fisherman's pie</u>

Curried prawns with pilau rice (*Indian*)

Moules marinière (*French*)

Meat

Beef goulash (*Hungarian*)

<u>Roast sirloin of beef with Yorkshire pudding</u>

<u>Steak and kidney pie</u>

Shish kebab (*Turkish and Arabic*)

Spare ribs Tex-Mex style (*American*)

Sweet and sour pork (*Chinese*)

<u>Baked ham with apricots</u>

Wiener schnitzel (*Austrian*)

<u>Roast pheasant with bread sauce</u>

<u>Game pie</u>

Osso buco (*Italian*)

Desserts

<u>Apple and blackberry crumble</u>

Crème caramel (*French*)

Apple strudel (*Austrian/German*)

<u>Rhubarb pie and custard</u>

<u>Treacle sponge pudding</u>

2   National cuisines tend to be based on ingredients and cooking methods that are commonly available in the country. Traditional British food reflects the wealth of fish, meat and dairy products available for many centuries. Hot, spicy dishes began to be eaten in the 18th century as a result of increased contact with India, and are now quite customary.

3   Students need not feel they must identify all the dishes at this stage. They can name others as they go through the unit.

> **ANSWERS**
>
> 1 shepherd's pie   2 haggis   3 fish and chips   4 smoked salmon   5 sandwiches   6 marmalade
> 7 scones   8 porridge   9 bangers (or sausages) and mash   10 roast beef & Yorkshire pudding
> 11 kippers   12 Cornish pasties   13 bacon and eggs   14 rice pudding

4   Pairs or groups. Students should enjoy hearing each other's experiences. If your students have not been to Britain, ask them if they have gathered any impressions about British food from books or films.

5   This is a fairly straightforward reading comprehension, but other uses might be made of these passages (dictation, gap-filling, etc.). Exercise 6 asks for a sentence based on A or B, but this could be extended to a paragraph or more; 'the framework for an autobiography' could lead to a more ambitious piece of writing; passages C and D might be used to construct a dialogue or argument between two opposing points of view.

Language notes:
A: 'umpteen' (colloquial) = many
B: 'charcutier' (French) = a high-quality butcher who sells fine cooked foods
C: 'a kind of soufflé': an odd description of this typical dish, Yorkshire pudding, which is a mixture of eggs, flour and milk, baked in the oven with hot fat from the roast.
D: 'the Puritans' = severe, moralistic, pleasure-avoiding Christians, who became the ruling power under Oliver Cromwell in the 17th century.
   'gridiron' = grill

> **ANSWERS**
>
> Suggested positions:
>
> | D | C | A B |
> |---|---|---|
> | **Very good** | **Mixed good & bad** | **Very bad** |

7   This exercise introduces the idea behind the game in exercise 8.

> **ANSWER**
>
> c (sausages in batter)

8 This is an amusing game, but it also calls for inventiveness and sensitivity to the language. The idea of 'Call My Bluff' is to make up definitions that are so plausible that the other players are fooled into accepting them as real. In some cases the name of a dish bears an obvious relation to the dish itself: 'jam roly poly' for instance is clearly derived from 'jam roll', and 'jugged hare' is hare cooked in a jug ('jug' here means a cooking pot). In other cases the connection is visual ('spotted dog') or associative ('shepherd's pie' is made with minced lamb).

ANSWERS

Jugged hare = hare stewed in a jug with onions and wine
Shepherd's pie = minced lamb covered with mashed potato and baked
Haggis wi' neeps and tatties (a traditional Scottish dish) = haggis (a sheep's stomach stuffed with liver and barley) with mashed swedes and potatoes
Bubble and squeak = fried onion, cabbage and potatoes
Devils on horseback = liver or prunes wrapped in bacon and grilled with hot pepper
Jam roly poly = a roll of pastry with jam sauce
Anglesey eggs = eggs with leeks, cream and melted cheese
Spotted dog = a pudding dotted with raisins
Lancashire hotpot = a casserole of potatoes, lamb and onions
Bangers and mash = sausages with mashed potato
Black pudding = a sausage made with blood, onions, oatmeal and fat
Cottage pie = minced beef covered with mashed potato and baked
Brandy snaps = ginger biscuits filled with cream and brandy
Scotch woodcock = a pyramid of toasted bread with anchovies, egg yolks and cream

---

3 CHANGING HABITS

1 A quiz to prepare students for some of the more surprising aspects of food and drink consumption in Britain. You could ask them to discuss the most interesting or surprising fact here. What are the social implications? Could the same thing be said of their country?

2 As there are two texts here, you will need to decide how to organise this activity. One way is to divide the class into pairs, and make each member of the pair A or B, who then read their text (A or B). Another way is to divide the class into two halves, A and B, who read accordingly. The comparison of the two texts thus becomes a reporting exercise between partners as well.

The aim of this exercise is for students to make deductions from information in the text. You may need to draw attention to the wording of the question: ... 'information that suggests a change in the way people *live*', i.e. not just in the way they eat. Students can be encouraged to speculate freely here, and to think about the way their lives are changing too. They should be gently urged to look beyond the obvious explanation: one social trend can have many causes. For example, increased consumption of frozen and convenience foods (ready cooked meals, etc.) may suggest that:

- people have more money.
- people have less time.
- convenience foods have improved.
- convenience foods are cheaper than they used to be.
- these foods are now marketed more cleverly than before.

Language notes:
As well as presenting different facts, there are interesting differences in stylistic register between the two texts, one an 'official' text full of administrative and statistical vocabulary – household consumption, nutrition, decline, etc. – and the other journalistic, with interviews, metaphors such as 'marching on their stomachs' (an ironic quote from Napoleon), 'stomach share', etc.

3 If you can provide statistics or survey data for precise comparisons, this will certainly be helpful. However a great deal can be done informally by students thinking about their own eating habits, changes in the types of food sold in local shops, new restaurants they have seen, and so on. They can also consult newspaper and magazine articles, family members and friends.

C | A TEENAGE DIET

1 *Language notes:*
Students should not worry about the exact meanings (or flavours) of all the foods mentioned. Many of them are part of the 'impressive arsenal of sweets and snacks' identified by the author of the *Guide Bleu* (passage C, page 33). Capitalised words are usually brand names.
Rice Krispies, Cornflakes, and Crunchy Nut Cornflakes are all breakfast cereals – often eaten at other times of the day.
Mars Bar and Kit Kat are chocolate and caramel bars. Glacier Mints are mint-flavoured sweets.
Wotsits and Monster Munch are savoury snacks similar to crisps.

ANSWERS

Pamela

Clues to the girl's identity are:
- she does not eat peanut butter and chocolate spread (so she is not Lucy)
- she does not eat 'lots of fruit and vegetables' and she is 'keen on sweets and crisps' (so she must be Pamela).

2 This could be extended as follows: the class is divided into groups of four. Each group submits one of their diets anonymously to another group, who then examine it and write a verdict on it. Anonymity should be protected for obvious reasons.

3

TAPESCRIPT

Unit 4C, exercise 3. Students from Edinburgh talk about what they eat.

I = Interviewer   B = Boy   B2 = Boy 2   B3 = Boy 3   G = Girl   G2 = Girl 2   G3 = Girl 3

I   So what do you eat for choice? Say, you're going out with a group of friends – admittedly you haven't got a lot of money to spend – but what would you go for? What sort of food would you go for?

B   Usually probably pizza. Maybe pizza, fish and chips, yeah, just your fish bars and your pizza shops, and pasta, quite a lot of pasta is eaten over here, quite a lot. Erm, that's mainly it.

I   Nobody's said hamburgers.

B2   Yeah but that's like an 'in town' thing, it's usually like for lunch as opposed to going out in the evening.

I   Sure. What I really meant to find out was what sort of food is most popular in your sort of group of friends?

B2   Probably fish and chips. And pizza as well.

G   Convenience foods. Like … places like McDonalds and Burger King have hamburgers and chips and that, they're just convenience foods really. I mean they taste great, but most folk just, just … I mean they're quick, they're fairly cheap, so you just go in, get out and out you go.

I   But do you think you have a different view of what you should eat compared to what your parents say? I mean you might say I want fish and chips and they say I'd rather you had, you know, salad and fresh fruit.

G2   … Not really. We'll sort of have fish and chips every so often, and then sort of a bit more healthy stuff in between. If we sort of all feel like just having a big junk food meal then we'll just get one in. And it's great.

I   But you don't, you don't … it doesn't become an issue at home?

G2   No. Not really.

I   Does it for you at all?

G3   Not an issue as such, but my folks, my parents are always saying oh you should eat more vegetables and I don't eat enough vegetables and fruit and all the rest of it. We don't … We're not exactly the junk food family, but certainly I enjoy the hamburgers and chips if I want to. But erm, no, I think it's important to have a sort of variety rather than just one set meal, you know. So it's not been a set issue, no.

I   Is it an issue where you live?

B3   Not really. We sort of have a very varied diet throughout the week but usually on the weekends, maybe on a Friday or a Saturday night, we might go out and have a Chinese meal or an Indian meal. We usually do that, but during the week it's just your average salads and … just a variety really.

You could begin by asking students a few questions: Have you ever eaten breakfast in Britain? What was it like? Where did you have it? Describe it to a partner, or to the class.

Students may well think of bacon and eggs as the 'typical' or 'traditional' British breakfast (this is still quite a common view in Britain), but how old is the tradition? The extract from Drummond and Wilbraham's book which students will read in exercise 6 provides an interesting corrective to the stereotype.

Language notes:
'Continental breakfast' = a European-style breakfast.

ANSWERS

Menu 1 is British. Menu 2 is Continental. Menu 3 is American.

---

6 This text is a reminder of how recently certain British traditions were established. Cross-cultural comparisons may well prove interesting here.

ANSWERS

18th century: cold meat, cheese, beer
19th century: some people: coffee or tea, rolls or toast
             wealthy people: porridge, fish, bacon, eggs, toast, marmalade
Today: a lighter and simpler type of meal

D HOSPITALITY

The cartoon at the top of page 40 shows several rules of good behaviour at a British table – most of them being broken. These rules are learned in childhood, and passed down the generations at family meals. Students may enjoy finding similar or contrasting rules in their cultures.

Hospitality also involves rules of behaviour, and the questions in exercise 1 are designed to make the transition from table manners to general rules of hospitality in a cross-cultural way.

2 Students may ask if the traditions described in this passage (written in the 1980s) are still rigidly observed today. They are not – at least not as widely as they once were. Rules of etiquette are, in any case, addressed to people who are concerned to behave correctly in the more formal strata of society. Anyone who behaved in this way would certainly be considered polite. (*Note:* the practice of not opening a bottle of wine which a guest brings, and then taking it to another party next week, is somewhat idiosyncratic, and not a standard rule.)

3 A reading comprehension which requires students to deduce cultural data from a narrative. Once students have done this, there are possibilities for more creative exploitation of the passage. For example:
- dramatisation
- writing a similar scene based in the student's country – this could be autobiographical or imaginary, in narrative or dramatic form
- a 'thank you' letter from Anita to Meena's parents
- an entry from Anita's diary about dinner at Meena's house

Meera Syal, the author of this passage, has become famous as a TV actor through starring in *Goodness Gracious Me,* a BBC comedy show based on Asian-British cultural contrasts. There is a photograph of her on page 18.

Language notes:

'empty-handed' = without a gift

'in shifts' = taking turns rather than all eating together (a 'shift' is normally a work-period)

'cat fight' = a noisy argument (as loud as cats fighting)

'fishfingers' = frozen fish sticks covered with breadcrumbs – a bland 'convenience food' often served to children

'chapatti' = unleavened Indian bread

ANSWERS

1   Anita is offended by the way Meena's family eat with their fingers, and by the Indian food they offer her.

2   Meena's family could be offended by the way that Anita comes to dinner empty-handed (she brings no gift), rejects their food, does not talk at table, and eats with her mouth open.

3   India: eating 'in shifts', not eating at a table, eating with fingers and using chapatti as scoops; a variety of spicy food (curries) with some plain foods (cheese and peas); good humour, generous hospitality.

England: eating at a table, with a knife and fork; suspicion of foreign foods; ignorance ('What's garlic?'); unsociable behaviour at table (although this is not typical).

EDUCATION

- To encourage critical reflection upon the goals of education
- To inform students about the evolution of primary, secondary and higher education in present-day Britain through a cross-cultural approach
- To give a flavour of daily life in British classrooms both through authentic interviews with students and through a fictional recreation in a recent play
- To invite students to compare what school life is like in Britain with their own experiences

GENERAL REMARKS

In Britain, schooling is compulsory from age five to sixteen and is free of charge, although some parents choose to send their children to fee-paying schools (the independent sector). Like so much in Britain today, education is a result of quite a complex history and today it is both in a state of transition and the subject of much controversy.

Until this century, there was no unified system of primary and secondary education in Britain, and compared to many other European countries, education was marked by a lack of direct, centralised government control. The 'public' schools (so called because anyone could send their children if they were able to pay the fees) like Eton, Harrow and Winchester gave their pupils (until recently boys) a largely classical education. Although fewer than 10% of children at primary or secondary level attend them today, fee-paying schools still play a role in British education as prestigious institutions educating many youngsters who later become prominent in public life.

In 1870, the Elementary Education Act made education for children from the ages of five to ten free and compulsory, but it was not until the 1944 Education Act that education became nationalised and obligatory in both primary and secondary schools.

Until the 1960s, children took tests when they were eleven, the results of which determined whether they would go to a 'grammar school' for the intellectually more able or a 'secondary modern' where the emphasis was much more on practical skills. In the 1960s, the majority of the grammar schools were abolished, giving way to comprehensive secondary schools. These still retained a large measure of autonomy, with each Head responsible for the school's curriculum. In the 1980s, however, the government, driven by fears that the standard of British education was relatively low, imposed a National Curriculum through the 1988 Educational Reform Act.

In this unit, parts A, B and C deal with primary and secondary education, while D examines the various educational provisions available for higher education.

A

WHAT DO SCHOOLS TEACH?

Before beginning the exercises, work with the visuals, asking students to describe them and discuss whether these photos remind them of any experiences they themselves had.

1 The unit begins from the student's own experiences. Going to school is something that the vast majority of people have undergone, which gives them a basis of fact and opinion from which to examine the education of another country. Students fill in the table to indicate the syllabus they followed in their primary and secondary years.

The questions ask them to think critically about their experiences. In small classes, they can be explored through a general discussion. In larger classes, it is often more productive to get students working in small groups, and then reporting their views to the class.

2 The National Curriculum was the first attempt in England and Wales (Scotland does not have this system) to centralise both the subjects students were taught in schools and to assess their progress at regular intervals. It may be useful to start by discussing with students their views on the necessity of such direct control by a government: is that the same in their country, and what are its possible benefits and drawbacks?

The comparison with the main subjects studied and with the goals for English can be done as a small group or whole class activity.

Language note:
'to forge ahead' = to make rapid progress

3 🞐🞐 Listening for gist and detail. Ask students to read the six sentences before they listen, and discuss any difficulties with them. Can they guess what DT stands for? If they find the recording difficult, play it in small sections – ask them to listen simply for the answer – e.g. for question 1, ask them to listen and pick out the two ages mentioned. This is useful training in picking out relevant information from within a flow of heard information.

Changing the sentences to make them appropriate for the student's own experience can be done orally as a class exercise or set as a written homework.

TAPESCRIPT
Unit 5A, Exercise 3. An interview with a teacher at a primary school.
T = Teacher   I = Interviewer

T   We have what we call Key Stage 1 assessment tasks for children, and that's at the end of seven years of age. Key Stage 2 are eleven years of age. And now you find that the girls are doing better at all key stages up to GCSE and A level. So it's a concern.

I   And can you tell us a bit more about the curriculum? … The National Curriculum …

T   Yes, well we've got, we're involved in a numeracy project, maths, and we've got a set amount of work for that. We've got a set amount of time set aside for English … because we want to give children who are actually coming out of school a number of basic skills in life, not just to get a job, you know, a variety of things. So we've got, so we have English and maths as the main subjects that we actually do in the morning. And the three core subjects are English, maths and science. And then we have a variety of other subjects which we support, RE, that's religious education, IT, information technology and DT, design technology, art, music, PE, that's physical education – and history, geography, all those subjects have to be included as well in the curriculum, you know, so the time scales are very, very tight. So we actually have a planned programme of work – topic work – to take into account history and geography, but it's very, very difficult to get everything done adequately, within the time that we have.

I And how many hours are the students, the pupils at school?

T Well we start 9 o'clock till 12, then 1 o'clock till quarter past 3. So that's the length … and five days a week.

ANSWERS

a 7, 11   **b** English, maths   **c** science   **d** design technology   **e** not enough time
f 12 (noon), 3:15pm (15:15), 5 days

B   WHAT ARE SCHOOLS LIKE?

1   The predicting exercise is important because it serves to deal with possible vocabulary or conceptual difficulties before students hear the interview.

TAPESCRIPT
Unit 5B, exercise 1. An interview with the Headmaster of Bablake school in Coventry.
H = Headmaster   I = Interviewer

H Well, if I start by saying that Bablake is an independent school, do you know what I mean by independent?

I Yeah, but it might be good if you tell us what exactly …

H OK. In England, there are in effect two types of school. There is a maintained school, which is really run by the local authority, which is responsible to the government, and then there is the independent school, which is really independent of local authority and to some extent independent of the government, and which is known as the fee-paying sector. So the parents who come, who send their children to Bablake will pay directly to the school, to have their children educated. So on that basis, as I say, Bablake is an independent school. We're also a selective school which means that parents who want their children to come here, I only take the children if they've passed an entry exam. And the children have to sit a verbal reasoning paper, an English paper and a maths paper and they also have to have a good report from their current headteacher, right? So we are, as I said, independent and selective. We're also a highly academic school, and our exam results are exceptionally high. We have nearly a hundred per cent pass rate at GCSE … I don't know if you're familiar with GCSE, at 16, and over 95% will go on to university. So it's very high. And I take really the top ten, maybe down to the top 15% of the academic range. So, you know, our standards are high, and the expectations of the pupils are that they will get good exam results, and then go on to university.

I Are most independent schools selective or …?

H The vast majority are selective. Some are more selective than others, because they can afford to be that way, and particularly day schools, which is what Bablake is, a day school. You also have some boarding independent schools and they tend – although there are again exceptions – but they tend to be less selective, because they don't have the choice. I have two, at least two girls and boys competing for every one place, so you know, there is competition to get into the school. And we are co-educational, which means that we have boys and girls here. A lot of independent schools tend to be single sex. They cater for girls or boys.

I Have you adopted the National Curriculum?

H We have to a certain extent, but the National Curriculum is fairly constraining in what you can offer, so what I say to parents is that we offer the National Curriculum, but also a lot more. And we try and gear our curriculum to the needs of the pupils. So we offer more languages, we offer more science, we offer, you know, more IT, more games, than a school that follows completely the national curriculum. But we have to follow very much what goes on in the national sector, because although we're independent, we are really part of the whole education system of Great Britain.

I Do you have many ethnic groups in your school?

H Yes, we do. Yes.

I How many?

H Seven or eight, I think. Yes … yes … don't quote me on that. We have … we have Hindus, we have Sikhs, we have Muslims, we've got Jews, we've got Afro-Caribbeans, we've got Chinese, so maybe we're up to about eight already on that basis. So there is at least 20% of the school population is of an ethnic group outside of Caucasian.

I Are they British … or British citizens?

H They regard themselves as being British citizens, yes. And you know, most of them are second generation or sometimes even third generation, so they regard themselves as being British … or English. Yes, yes, very much so. And they're actually quite proud … I mean they're proud to be British, but they're also proud of what they are, you know Hindu, or Muslim or Sikh, or … or whatever.

I And do you have to take this very much into account in the organisation of the school? I mean, are there any special arrangements, say for Muslims, or …

H No. No, we don't really make any special consideration. I mean, they come to the school for an education, they don't really come to school for religious purposes. So we are a Christian foundation, but we recognise the other ethnic groups and their religion, and we teach all the children about the different ethnic groups and their various religions. But I think once you start to make (*coughs*) … excuse me … special arrangements, then you start to highlight one particular group. So, you know we will celebrate special occasions, so … you know the festival of light, Diwali, the Jewish New Year, the Chinese New Year, all of these occasions will be mentioned. And we will celebrate them as a whole school, simply by acknowledging them. But … and well that's really the only special occasions and special thing that we do.

ANSWERS

1 They pass entry exams in verbal reasoning, English and maths, and have to have a good report from their current headteacher.

2 Nearly 100% success at GCSE, over 95% of students go on to university.

3 Bablake is a day school rather than a boarding school, it can therefore be more selective (it has at least two students competing for each place) and it is co-educational, taking both boys and girls.

4 At least 7 or 8, 20% of the students, Hindus, Sikhs, Muslims, Jews, Afro-Caribbeans, Chinese.

2 Reasons for or against can be listed on the board. These can obviously be used as the basis for a debate or a written essay of opinion.

3 ▭ Students can record their descriptions on their own and then play them to a partner or a small group to compare their opinions.

TAPESCRIPT
Unit 5B, exercise 3. A Scottish student talks about his school.
I = *Interviewer*   A = *Alastair*

I Tell me about your school, please.

A It's a large school. Holds about 1,200 pupils. The teachers are on the whole friendly but there's the odd exception. The pupils, it's … comes from quite a wide base. There's a few different cultures here but everyone seems to get on quite well. There's not too much aggro, there's not too much fighting or anything. So, I mean it's a good school, it's got quite a good tradition and a high standard of education. It's quite renowned for being pretty good at sports: like rugby and football.

ANSWERS

Important aspects: a large school, teachers on the whole friendly, different cultures but everyone seems to get on quite well, not too much aggressiveness or fighting, it's got a good tradition, a high standard of education, and pretty good at sports: rugby and football.

aggro = **c** violence

4 This is designed to act as a pre-reading task to bring out the issues and vocabulary before students listen. It is usually better to start the discussion work in pairs or small groups as the larger group or the presence of the teacher may inhibit some students from giving their true opinions.

5 Encourage reading quickly for gist. Students shouldn't worry too much about unfamiliar words in this first reading, but simply read to do the fairly easy matching task.

ANSWERS

1B   2C   3A   4D

6 In this exercise, students re-read the texts and identify the issues mentioned. The final question is a way of eliciting their reaction. Ask them to say why they found the opinion interesting – is it similar to theirs, or does it give an insight into a different kind of schooling compared with their own, etc.?

ANSWERS

School clothing; bullying; exams; differences in achievement between boys and girls; relations with teachers.

7 Again, a pre-listening exercise, to work with the vocabulary and the concepts beforehand. Students could work in small groups to establish the qualities they think most important in teachers.

ANSWERS

1d 2f 3b 4e 5a 6c

8 Discussing their own views in the previous exercise has set up the cultural comparison requested here. All the expressions in the speech bubbles in exercise 7 can be ticked! A class feedback might be to list the main differences between the Bristol students' views and those of the class.

TAPESCRIPT

Unit 5B, exercise 8. Five students choose the most important qualities in a teacher.

I = Interviewer 1–5 = Students 1–5

I What do you think is the most important quality in a teacher?

1 I think it's someone who you can respect, but who isn't too intimidating.

2 I think getting the point across, really. Explaining things simply. 'Cause otherwise you're never going to learn anything I mean.

3 I would say the ability to communicate what he wants to teach you in a way which makes you interested. And in theory, that should mean that his personality doesn't have to be quite so important.

4 I think it's approachability. If you've got a problem, I really think you should be able to go up to the teacher and say 'Look, I've got a problem' and then expect the teacher to help you. Also, you've got to have a teacher who sort of inspires you, inspires confidence – his techniques are good. They're the most important qualities for me. Someone who you can get on with but is teaching you, teaching you well, and he's not teaching down to you.

5 The teacher himself has to be good. But also it really ought to be ... he ought to be a sort of nice person that you can trust or talk to.

C **WHAT ARE CLASSES LIKE?**

Babies is by Jonathan Harvey, a young English playwright who was brought up in Liverpool and then worked as a teacher in London. It was first performed in 1994 at the Royal Court, the theatre in London which puts on the greatest number of experimental plays as well as plays by young or unknown writers.

Notes about the scene:

The extract is taken from the opening of the play and shows many aspects that are typical of life in many British schools. The teacher, Joe, is 'taking the register' – a formal exercise required at the beginning of the day in English schools, in which the teacher calls out the name of the pupils in turn, and they indicate that they are present. The column on the left represents the names as Joe calls them out (the stage direction indicates that students answer 'here', 'yeah' and 'yo Sir'. ('Yeah' and 'yo' are slang variations of 'yes'.) The right-hand column reproduces the chatter of the students while the register is being taken. As shown in this scene, a male teacher would be referred to as 'Sir' (while a female one, regardless of her marital status, would most often be called 'Miss').

Joe addresses his class collectively as '9CY' (many schools identify a class by a number and the initials of its class tutor). He uses informal language, like 'Yeah?' (a more formal teacher might say something like 'Is that understood?') or 'dead sad' (= very sad, 'dead' being a slang intensifier popular with young people). He also has some dialectal pronunciation, e.g. 'yous' for you.

If students don't notice, point out that Joe's comments show him adhering to a 'code of conduct' which could be either personal – e.g. he doesn't allow derogatory statements about members of staff in his classroom, nor gossip about a person's sexual orientation – or imposed by the school, which prohibits physical contact between staff and students. When they misbehave, students can be sent to the Headteacher or some other figure of authority (here Miss Sterry). Many schools in Britain do not allow the students to wear make-up (at least before the sixth form) and most prohibit smoking in school. Simone wears mascara and has Bensons (a brand of cigarette) and a lighter in her handbag. These details could be taken to show that the school, in a rather deprived part of London, does not apply this kind of rule too stringently.

Language notes:
'Head' = a fashionable manufacturer of sports accessories
'over the moon' (idiomatic) = extremely pleased
'taking the mickey' (slang) = mocking, making a joke of something that is supposed to be serious
'a moany old cow' (slang, very disrespectful) = a stern or disagreeable person
'In'e a blinding teacher, eh?' (pronunciation and slang) = Isn't he a wonderful teacher?

Notes about the activities:

Reading a play 'on the page' is always a much less interesting experience than actually seeing it or, better still, performing it. The drama activities suggested in exercise 1 are simple but powerful ways of allowing the students to create their personal interpretation of the play or adapt it creatively to their own ideas and views.

The first option, a dramatic reading, brings the play to life in the classroom and is usually more effective than a straightforward reading by the teacher or the traditional reading aloud 'in turn'. Students can prepare it in groups and compare their interpretations afterwards. Even a minimal staging will allow students to get 'inside' the scene and understand it much more intimately than before. It also helps them to read the lines with the required emotional colouring, which is quite useful phonological practice.

The other two options call for more time and preparation and they could be done as a more extended project, following the first dramatic reading and discussion of the play. The second option suggests writing a scene for the play – but it would also be possible to improvise the scene. Performing it for the class can be very enjoyable both for the group itself, and for spectators in the class.

D WHAT HAPPENS AFTER SECONDARY SCHOOL?

1 Start by describing and discussing the photos, which show young people following two different career routes after secondary school: being trained as apprentices for a practical trade, or going on to some form of higher education. Students may respond by talking about their own experiences, ambitions, hopes.

The flow chart can be discussed as a whole class exercise. If there are quite a few differences between Britain and their own country, students in groups choose the option of creating a flow chart of their own.

2

ANSWERS

1 Education   2 Youth training   3 Employment

3 This serves as a pre-reading exercise, to get students to think about the topic, the procedure needed to gain entry into university, as well as to familiarise them with some of the vocabulary in the article which follows.

The more specialised vocabulary is explained briefly in the six statements. If 'open days' are not part of the experience of students, explain that many universities nowadays give sixth-form students an opportunity to visit the campus. On the designated day, students can tour the whole university, listen to talks about the university's facilities and the various courses offered, and meet some of the tutors and students in their particular areas of interest.

4 It may be useful to ask students to note the breezy, informal style of the diary entries (e.g. 'plodding on' for 'continuing to work') similar to the language of the playscript in part C, and contrast it with the more formal registers of the government brochure (p. 43) and the newspaper articles (p. 45).

ANSWERS

c   a   d   f   d   b   e (implied)

5 The suggested options can be used as homework.

LEISURE

AIMS

- To provide students with information about what people do in their free time in Britain and invite comparisons
- To give an idea of contemporary British television, cinema and theatre
- To elicit the students' own opinions about various leisure pursuits and compare them with their British equivalent

GENERAL REMARKS

This unit examines some leisure activities in today's Britain, and in particular television, cinema and the theatre. As in other units, the focus is on lifestyles and individual choices rather than on institutions, although a brief glance is also cast upon television programmes available in Britain, the current development of the film industry, and the variety of theatres in England and Scotland.

A WHAT DO YOU DO IN YOUR FREE TIME?

1 In larger classes, this is best be done as a group activity, with each group making their lists on the board.

2 Doing the first guessing activity in pairs leads to greater discussion of the issues involved. Students will later (exercise 5) be asked to comment on the survey and the listening exercises which follow.

3 ▭▭ Listening for specific items. Ask students to read the list of activities before they listen, discuss any difficulties, and, once again, compare with their own lives. If your class finds listening difficult, play the interviews in sections, stopping after each speaker, then let them listen to the whole without interruption. In some cases, the activity is mentioned by more than one student.

Note: The first speaker says that Bristol is the second biggest city in England, which is not quite true. Although it is the largest city in southwestern England, its population is smaller than London, Birmingham, and Manchester.

ANSWERS

a 2 **b** 1, 2, 3 **c** 1, 3 **d** 3 **e** 3 **f** 1 **g** 2 **h** 2 **i** 3 **j** 3

TAPESCRIPT

Unit 6A, exercise 3. Students in England talk about how they use their free time.

I = Interviewer   1–3 = Students

I If your lessons finish around lunch time or early afternoon, what do you do with the rest of the day?

1 It depends, really. Now that we're in our final year there's always quite a lot of work to do but apart from that we're right next to Clifton, which is like a village, so we can go in there, go to cafés, go to shops, and then it's not far to go into Bristol – get the bus, or you can walk if you wanted, and I mean with it being the second biggest city in England you've got every shop you can imagine.

2 Well, recently spare time has become a little non-existent. But I do quite a lot of music. And socialising and I mean basically this year there's a lot more work and a lot more organisation to do so there isn't very much during the school day. I mean there are quite often large gaps. The school day is structured so that there are large gaps between lessons sometimes but in practice you tend to have to work or do something else in that time.

3 I've got a lot of work to do outside of actual classes, I've got a lot of homework to do. Then there are extra things like preparing essays for the Internet – our Internet website. I have to prepare an essay for geography and an essay for Spanish every now and again and also I'm, well I'm part of the catering committee so I have to do quite a bit of work for that – and various responsibilities within the house. Socially, going up to Clifton village, shopping, things like that. Every now and again a bit of sport if I'm lucky. But generally it's a lot of work, and you're just trying to get some free time to relax and unwind really, and get up and get yourself away from the pressures of everyday school life.

4 ▭▭ This time the students listen to take notes. Working in pairs lightens the amount of writing each student has to do. If it is useful, play the tape a second time and let each pair help each other to complete gaps.

Language notes:
Speaker 3 talks about performing with her music band at ceilidhs (a Gaelic word pronounced 'kaylies') which are evenings of Scottish or Irish music and dance.
'on the odd occasion' = from time to time, not too often

ANSWERS

1 go out with friends; watch videos, chat, listen to music, go to the cinema; spend time with girlfriend

2 go to a friend's house, meet others, watch videos, sometimes go to the cinema or go driving

3 go out with friends, practise or perform with a band; go to the cinema, or stay home to watch videos

4 go out with boyfriend, sometimes with other friends or to a friend's house

TAPESCRIPT

Unit 6A, exercise 4. Students from Scotland describe what they do on Saturday evenings.

I = Interviewer   S1 = Student 1   S2 = Student 2   S3 = Student 3   S4 = Student 4

I So tell me David, what would you be doing on a typical Saturday evening?

S1 Either going out with my friends or visiting a friend, going to the cinema or perhaps spending some time with my girlfriend.

I If you go out with your friends, where do you go?

S1 Usually to each other's houses, watch videos, sit around and chat, listen to music. I used to be in a band and I spent quite a lot of time rehearsing and playing with those but it's not really worked out so we don't do that any more.

I How about you? What do you do on a Saturday night, typically?

S2 Just mainly the same. Usually just go round to a few friends' houses, just meet up, watch videos, occasionally go out to the cinema ... and go out sometimes driving, 'cause I've just passed my driving test.

S3 Yeah, I'm usually out with my friends. Or I'm also in a band. But it's a Scottish music band and we need to practise an awful lot. And we've usually got a few engagements, like concerts or various ceilidhs to do, so that's good fun and usually we go to the cinema or just stay home, just watch video with friends, whatever.

S4 I'll either be out with my boyfriend or if we've got some money we'll be out, go somewhere in town with friends or go round to someone's house.

I Do any of you go to clubs or discos at all?

S4 Not really.

S3 On the odd occasion.

5 Comparison and discussion. Encourage students to comment on, for example, the predominance of television (and video) in both the survey and the students' replies; the relative importance of reading, gardening or playing with pets in the survey (not mentioned by the students) the balance between active versus more passive activities in the survey and the students' answers; the absence of participation in sports as a weekly event in the survey, etc.

6
7 These build upon the previous discussion, focusing specifically on opinions about television, and preparing for the following exercise, 8. There are no right and wrong answers to the listing of advantages and disadvantages. Amongst advantages, students might list: viewers can get a lot of information about the world; they can be entertained; they can see productions of plays, concerts, ballet, operas that they might not be able to see if they don't live in the capital or can't afford them; they can hear contrasting views and opinions on important issues, etc. Amongst disadvantages: watching is a sedentary activity, and too much could be unhealthy; there is not enough time left for reading, academic work, sports, etc.; there might be inappropriate, trivial, or disturbing programmes; television advertisements could be misleading, etc.

8 The poem is an extreme view designed to provoke response! Encourage students to read it out loud to each other right through, without worrying too much if some words or expressions are unfamiliar – the general message will surely come across very clearly. In addition, many words, like the ones in the line: 'They loll and slop and lounge about' (all expressions indicating relaxed, sloppy sitting) become clear through the context even if they were not known before.

9 A follow-up activity that can be set as homework. If at all possible, pin up the results – it is enjoyable for students to read and compare poems or letters written by others.

TELEVISION

The world of British television has changed greatly since the BBC (the British Broadcasting Corporation) started broadcasting the world's first regular television service in 1936. The BBC had been chartered by Parliament in 1927 to be the sole provider of British broadcasting. It was never under direct government control, but is managed by a board of Governors and a Director General. There is no commercial sponsorship, the service being financed by an annual licence fee paid by everyone who owns a television set. The first Director General, Lord Reith, identified the mission of the BBC as threefold: to educate, to entertain and to inform. The BBC opened its second channel in 1964, but its monopoly of television broadcasting had already ended in 1954 when Parliament established the Independent Television Authority (ITA) a consortium of regional companies now known as Channel 3. Later developments included the establishment of two new terrestrial channels, Channels 4 and 5, the commercial operation of a series of satellite channels and the recent introduction of digital television. Despite the proliferation of commercial channels, British viewers must still obtain an annual licence to support the BBC.

The end of the previous section focused on television viewing habits. In B, students are invited to think about the kinds of programmes that are available and how they are made.

A vocabulary building exercise that ends with an exchange of views about preferences. This may lead to a discussion of the kinds of programmes that are made and shown in the students' own country. If satellite transmission from Britain is available, some extracts from programmes can be shown with students asked to give their opinion about them.

ANSWERS
a 3   b 10   c 1   d 7   e 2   f 9   g 8   h 5   i 4   j 6

Pre-reading discussion, to set the scene for the texts that follow. If students are interested, they could work in groups to produce either a more fully worked-out proposal for a TV programme, or the script for it.

3   1   Pre-reading. If students cannot think of many factors which could make the production process relaxed or stressful, ask them to consider the following variables:

- time constraints: is the production likely to be rushed, or leisurely?
- financial constraints: is the cost of various options likely to be decisive?
- commercial constraints: are the sponsors of the programme likely to exert pressures on the people producing it?
- political or other pressure-group constraints: are the makers likely to be influenced by the possibility of either pleasing or displeasing powerful interests in society?
- the personality of the director and the actors: what kind of reputation do these people have – that of being easy to work with, or very temperamental and hard to please?

2   Reading the texts. Students work either in pairs, with each one reading one text and then comparing their reactions, or they read one text after the other. Ask students to give their overall response to the two extracts before moving on to the detailed questions about them.

3   The extracts. These are from recent novels, and both portray people in the media business talking the kind of specialised 'media-slang' that is typical of the industry.

Notes about the authors and books:

Malcolm Bradbury (b. 1932) is a prominent English author of novels, short stories, critical works and plays. His first book, *Eating People is Wrong* (1959) and the popular *The History Man* (1975), which was adapted for television, were both satires on university life. *Cuts* (1987) is a short, comic, satirical novel about life in the television industry.

Helen Fielding is a young journalist and novelist, born in Yorkshire, who worked for many years for the BBC. *Bridget Jones's Diary* began life as a serialised column in a national newspaper, then was on the best-seller lists for months when it was published as a book in 1997. Its protagonist is a young woman who records her daily struggle trying to lose weight, stop smoking, and find both a satisfying job and a satisfying love life.

Language notes:

'stain the pavement' = be killed in a bloody mess on the pavement – an example of Lord Mellow's excessive metaphorical style!

'shredded, pulped' = completely destroyed

'slide down the pole': fire stations often have a central pole down which the firemen can slide quickly when the alarm goes

'on my cue' = when the director tells the reporter to start

'Go, go, go Newcastle': the director is indicating the order in which reports are to be televised – first the report from Newcastle, while Bridget is waiting, 'standing by', then her report from Lewisham in London

ANSWERS

1 **A** a historical drama **B** a documentary

2 Lord Mellow and Richard Finch both come across as bullies, sure of their own importance, not very sensitive to people around them, intent on getting the programmes made in their own way at whatever personal cost to others.

3 There is no right or wrong answer to this question, but many people might find the experience highly stressful.

C CINEMA

1 A light-hearted warm-up to the theme. The visuals show a mixture of older 'classic' films and actors, and a few more recent successes. Encourage students to do the matching exercise quickly, asking for help from others and not worrying too much if they don't know some of the photos or stills. They are meant as an aid to the discussion of films that the students have seen and what they thought of them.

ANSWERS

a The Pink Panther   **b** From Russia With Love   **c** The Full Monty   **d** Shirley Valentine
e Sense and Sensibility   **f** Gandhi   **g** Helena Bonham Carter   **h** Emma Thompson
i Kate Winslet   **j** Elizabeth Taylor   **k** Anthony Hopkins   **l** Alec Guinness   **m** Michael Caine
n Kenneth Branagh

2 A whole class discussion, or a 'pyramid' exercise; students in pairs discuss their ideas, then join another pair, then another. One person from each larger group then reports the main points of their discussion to the whole class.

3 🔲 Listening for detail, set as a listening puzzle. Students transfer the grids on to their notebooks, leaving room to take notes. They listen once or twice if necessary, then compare the notes they've taken and, in pairs or small groups, work out the name of each student by taking account of the clues. The names can be found by a process of deduction and elimination. For example, clue 1 means that speakers 1 and 6 can be either Kay or Sheena, and either 2 or 5 could be Bill. However, 5 also says he goes to the cinema quite regularly, so he must be Bill (clue 3). And so on. The completed grid, with names, is given below.

Language note:

the 'Showcase' = the name of a large 'multiplex' set of cinema theatres, of the kind which are increasingly found in the suburbs of any fair-sized city in Britain

ANSWERS

Number	How often?	What kind of film?	Time problem?	Money problem?	Name?
1	quite a bit		Yes	Yes	Kay
2	quite often, once a month		Yes	No	Simon
3	not often	films with good reviews			Alex
4	doesn't go much, once a month	big spectacular films			Paul
5	quite regularly		No	No	Bill
6	quite often	comedies and action films			David
7	quite regularly	comedies		Yes	Sheena

TAPESCRIPT
Unit 6C, exercise 3. Students from England and Scotland say how often they go to the cinema.

I = Interviewer   1–7 = Students

 I   Do you go to the cinema, and if so, how often on average?

 1   I like going to the cinema, actually. I don't have so much time, some of the cinemas around Bristol can be quite expensive, especially the ones where they show all the films, like the Showcase. It's got so many screens but it costs so much, there's just no point. But yeah, I like films a lot. I go quite a bit with my friends.

 2   I go to the cinema quite often, not as often as I used to, because I don't have very much free time apart from weekends, during which time I'm down the pub. So ... but I like going to films when I can. On Sundays, perhaps, once every month or something.

 3   I don't tend to go to the cinema very much. I only tend to go when there's something which either has a very good review or something I think I will enjoy, so I don't tend to go very much.

 4   Yeah, I don't ... I'm not a great cinema goer, probably sort of once a month or something, I just see the big spectacular films in the cinema, just the major releases, really.

5 Quite regularly. Not everybody goes as often as me because I work in a cinema. So I can get in for free, pretty much whenever I want. So I've seen almost every film that's come out in recent times.

6 Yeah, I do go to the cinema quite often. I quite like comedies. They're quite … they're pretty good. And I also like action films. They're pretty good as well.

7 Yes, I go quite regularly with friends when I've got the money, 'cause you know the prices vary quite a lot. I saw *Titanic* recently as well and I thought it was really good. I really enjoy, I enjoy comedies and things like that so *The Full Monty* was really good, probably the best film I saw last year.

4 This is set as a comparative exercise. Students may not know any of the answers, in which case they could be set the task of finding out as much as they can about their country's cinema industry (by consulting books, newspapers, the Internet, etc.) before the next class, when they share their information. They can then compare with the facts given about Britain, on page 93.

5 Films are often interpreted as emblems of a whole society, e.g. *Pulp Fiction, Four Weddings and a Funeral*. If students can't think of a suitable film, they can be set an alternative task, of listing the 'ingredients' that they would include if they were making a film about their country: e.g. what locations would they choose? What kind of people (trades, professions, etc.) would the film show? Would the film be fictional, or a documentary? If the former, what kind of plot would they favour?

6 Listening for gist and details. Reading the questions beforehand can help with comprehension. The interview is a long one – if your students find it difficult, play the recording in sections, stopping before the interviewer asks another question – let them jot down answers, and then play a second time right through.

Notes about the films:
Tim Fywell's most recent films for television include *Madame Bovary* (1999); *Bad Blood* (a three-part series by Tony Marchant, 1998/99); *Touch and Go* (1998); *The Woman in White* (1997); and *The Ice House* (1996–7). His work in the theatre included plays at the Royal Court: *Red Saturday* by Martin Allen and *Spring Awakening* by Frank Wedekind; at the Riverside Studios: *The Mother Country* by Hanif Kureishi; and at the National Theatre, where he wrote and directed *No Hand Signals*.

Language notes:
'basic rudiments' = the elementary knowledge needed
'the best train set a boy could ever have': note the rather playful irony of suggesting that directing is really like a child's game, and also possibly the gendered bias of Orson Welles' remark – Orson Welles was a famous director working at a time before there were many women directors, when the film industry was largely dominated by men
'interference from on high' = interference from the director's superiors, higher management, etc.
'put in their two pennyworth' (familiar) = give their own opinions
'too many cooks spoil the broth (familiar) = too many people interfering with a project will produce a worse result
'breathing down your neck' (colloquial) = interference, excessive supervision
'the casting process' = the process of choosing actors
'hassle' (slang) = irritating interference

ANSWERS

1 He did a directing course with the BBC.

2 *The Samurai* by Melville.

3 Being in control of the whole 'vision' of the film, including script, actors, shots, camera angles, design. Also having a chance to put his vision of life on screen. Quoting Orson Welles, he compares a film director to a child with a wonderful toy. He also says it is exciting and challenging.

4 Interference by executive producers and TV companies. Compromise.

5 In America directors are better paid, but there is more interference by the studio, which is very powerful; money is everything. Britain is moving in the same direction, but film-makers still have more freedom.

6 *Cuts* seems a little old-fashioned in tone but is generally true: changing fashions mean sudden changes of mind, and money (represented by audience viewing figures) is far more important than truth or quality. He is amused by *Bridget Jones' Diary*, and thinks it accurately portrays the 'nerves and speed' of live documentary television, although this is a separate area of TV which he does not know well.

TAPESCRIPT
Unit 6C, exercise 6. An interview with the film director Tim Fywell.

I = Interviewer   TF = Tim Fywell

I How did you become a film director?

TF I worked in the theatre for years after I left university. I worked in theatre working on new plays with new writers, and that was satisfying up to a point, but financially not very rewarding, and also new plays particularly tended to be seen in by very small audiences in small venues. So I was always attracted to the idea of working in film and television, but it took a long time to make the transition from theatre to TV. Eventually I got on a thing called the BBC Directors' Course which was for both people that are working in TV in other jobs, maybe cameramen that wanted to direct, and also they used to have two places a year for theatre directors. So at the third time of applying I managed to get on this course, after very rigorous interviews. And that was as I say about a three-month course which taught one the basic rudiments of directing.

I Is there a particular film that you're inspired by? I mean do you have a favourite film made by another director?

TF I suppose I have quite a lot of favourite films, and before starting any work on any particular film of my own I'll tend to look at other people's films, you know, that maybe have some connection with the film that I'm making or that inspire me. I mean one film that I really like that I've watched over and over again is a French film called *The Samurai* by a director called Melville, and stars an actor called Alain Delon. Basically there's not a lot of dialogue in the film, he plays a kind of hitman, an assassin, and you see him in his apartment in Paris, and then you see him carrying out various jobs, you don't see very much emotion in him but he falls in love with this woman pianist in a night club and so he actually breaks his rules of professionalism and goes to see her and that's when he gets killed, at the end of the film. But it's a very haunting film, told very much through pictures and music, and very atmospheric of Paris and beautifully acted. That's one of my favourite films.

I Is there anything you particularly like about your job?

TF Ordering people around? Being in control! (*laughs*) Being the boss, telling people what to do ... Yeah, I do enjoy all that but I think, I mean more seriously than that I think it's being sort of in control of your ... you are in control of the film not just by telling people what to do but you're in control of the whole kind of vision of the film, the actors that you choose, trying to get the script right with the writer, helping the actors to find their performances, choosing all the shots, the camera angles, you know, discussions with the designer, the cameraman, so it's very much a chance to put your kind of vision of the world, or a particular bit of the world, on the screen. So it's a very exciting job, it's what Orson Welles said: the best train set that a boy could ever have. And it is.

I Is there anything you dislike about your job?

TF I suppose not many things, because, I mean I feel very lucky to do a job like this, which is enormously exciting and challenging. I think what I dislike maybe is ... I think there's more and more ... as programme-makers or film studios get more nervous about the amount of money that their programmes or films are going to make, there's more and more interference from on high in the film-maker's rôle. You don't now go to a script meeting just with a writer, there tend to be two or three executive producers there and everybody's got to put in their two pennyworth, and so it can become a case of too many cooks spoiling the broth, and you know and just annoying things like films have to be cut down to a certain length sometimes just to fit certain kind of – especially on TV – certain time-slots which may not be the actual right length for that film, so you know there is a fair amount of compromise involved. But those are the areas I dislike.

I And I know that you've made films in the United States as well as in Britain. What would you say are the main differences, in your experience, between making films in America and making films in Britain?

TF Well I think it's really to amplify the point that I just made. I mean England is becoming more like America in that respect, but in America, well certainly my experience of filming there was the power of the studio which was making the film, they had an enormous amount of power, and even though as a director you have quite a lot of freedom, in that case you just felt these people kind of breathing down your neck. And they were incredibly involved in the casting process and the editing process, and they kept changing their minds as to exactly what kind of film they were looking for, so one felt a bit, you know, inhibited. One's hands were tied by them. And although in England theoretically it's a lot freer than that, one has a lot more freedom, but I think it's going the way of America more – without the same amount of money being involved obviously. So one of the benefits of working in America is you get paid better, but you get a lot more interference and hassle. It's not really ... certainly Hollywood is not ... it sounds like the paradise for film-makers but really it's not a film-maker's place it's a film production place, and all that counts is how many dollars a film is going to make.

I What do you think of this scene from *Cuts* by Malcolm Bradbury?

TF I think, I mean it's slightly old-fashioned in its tone – I can see it's written in 1987 – but I would say the gist of it is true, in the sense ... I mean obviously it's a kind of satire on the way that a television company works in that the chief executive is looking for scapegoats amongst his staff as to why this particular project is not working the way he thought he would. Also I think what is true about it is the sense of people changing their minds almost overnight: what's commercial yesterday suddenly isn't commercial today, so they want a completely different idea, and what's commercial today may not be commercial tomorrow. It's a satire on what I was talking about before, the idea of really you know what counts in this case is pulling in the viewing figures, and so they're desperately searching around for something that they think will work. Whether it's actually truthful or good or dramatic or not is irrelevant.

I   And what about *Bridget Jones's Diary*?

TF Well, that's a very amusing piece. I mean I know less about that because it's talking about a documentary reporter and that's not an area that I've ever worked in, but I think the ... it conveys the kind of feeling of nerves and pressure of somebody new starting a job like that and are they going to make a go of it or are they going to mess it up, and, yeah, I think it conveys very well the sort of nerves and speed of live television, but as I say it's not the kind of work that I do, the films that I make, it's in a different area. Every area of TV is very separate, I think: drama, news, comedy, documentaries, they're all very separate kind of worlds. But as far as I can tell it's accurate as a satire on the world of news reporters.

I   Are directors ... Are most directors that you know tyrants in the way that they are portrayed here as well?

TF I think you've got to be a little bit of a tyrant, but I mean hopefully one can be a sort of ... pleasant tyrant.

D | THEATRE

In this section, information about the variety of theatres in England and Scotland is conveyed in the form of a simulation exercise. This is quite a large-scale activity and it may need more than one class session to prepare and perform it.

A possible way of organising this is as follows:

1 Students in groups study the texts, which are all from guide books to Britain. They are authentic texts, written in a colloquial style, which may present some lexical problems. Some help with vocabulary is given in each case, but encourage students to guess some other unknown words from the context. (For example, text A tells students that London has a 'plethora' of major stages. The context can help students to tell that 'a plethora of' = a lot of.) If necessary, some of this work can be done in class and the finalising continued as homework.

2 Students together make a list of the major attractions of the town in the text they've read.

3 They discuss ways of presenting these main attractions in a convincing way. Remind them of techniques used in advertising and other persuasive texts. What can they say to make their weekend sound irresistible?

4 They present their proposals to the other groups.

5 Round up and feedback for the exercise can take different forms, depending on the interests of your class.

   • A vote amongst the groups for the most attractive proposal can sometimes be enjoyable.

   • Comparing and discussing the persuasive strategies used can be useful for some groups.

- Students are asked to respond to the possibilities for theatre outlined in the texts they've read or heard about. What would be most interesting for them personally? What is their experience with theatre-going? Which plays have they seen recently? Did they enjoy it?
- Students are asked to compare the theatre in their own country: do they think that theatre is important in their national culture? Is there a lively tradition of local and fringe drama productions?
- Alternatively, this comparative exercise can be set up as a project: Students find guides to theatres in their country and prepare a similar simulation exercise, as though for English students visiting. They may use the English texts as guidance for translating some key ideas or passages from guide books written in their own language.

Language notes:
London
'a vast array' = a great number
'vibrant' (the comedy scene) = lively, with many things happening
'crop up' = appear
'disgorge a stream' = continuously produce a number of
'have been hijacked' = have been completely taken over (by musicals)
Stratford-upon-Avon
'a constant diet of' = nothing but
The Edinburgh Festival
'large-scale operation serving an annual influx of … acts' = a large organisation which every year has many acts from elsewhere
'from the inspired to the truly diabolical' = from very good to very bad!

Picture notes:
page 57: The National Theatre and a Victorian West End theatre.
page 58: (*left to right*) The Shakespeare Centre, The Royal Shakespeare Theatre, Anne Hathaway's Cottage.
Page 59: The Royal Mile, during the Festival.

2 The section and the unit end on a creative note, with students asked to imagine the play in 'the smallest theatre in the world'. If they enjoy drama work, they could improvise a 'smallest theatre' in their classroom to perform their short dialogues or monologues.

NEWSPAPERS, MAGAZINES, BOOKS

AIMS

- To provide information and stimulate comparative discussion about the print media in Britain today
- To increase students' awareness and critical assessment of their own relationship with newspapers, magazines and books
- To encourage discussion of contemporary issues

GENERAL REMARKS

Newspapers, magazines and books offer valuable opportunities for examining a culture in the process of change.

We begin with magazines, mainly examples that are popular with 16–18 year-olds in Britain. These will inevitably have similarities to the youth magazines of other countries. Although some students dislike attempts on the part of teachers to cross over into their territory, we hope that the chance to work with familiar materials in a personal way will provide a helpful entry route to a very complex and protean topic.

On newspapers, there is a focus on the divisions between 'quality', 'middle market' and 'popular' newspapers. This is only one of the distinctive features of the British press, but it is characteristic and suggests possibilities for comparisons to be made with other countries. In this part of the chapter, too, we are dealing with material that goes very rapidly out of date. Since British newspapers are easy to buy or consult in many parts of the world, we hope that teachers will feel motivated to integrate or update the work in this chapter with their own materials. Comparison of British newspapers with those in the learner's culture, particularly over the same topical news stories, can be of great interest.

A   READING HABITS

1   Exploring the covers is probably best done with students discussing in small groups, then reporting either to the roving teacher or to the rest of the class. This offers an opportunity for students to express their preferences in a relaxed way but it's also a chance for the teacher to find out more about what the students are really interested in – without asking directly.

2   Students can write individually. It's then useful for students to talk about their own questionnaires with others before they go on to compare with the British students in the next exercise.

3 Students discuss similarities or differences in groups of three or four and then talk about the kind of person each British student might be. There are no right or wrong answers – this is simply a way of exploring the question of whether people's reading habits can reveal something of their personality, the things they consider important, their lifestyle, etc. Afterwards, groups report the main or most interesting points of their discussion to the class.

Notes:

There are additional notes on *The Big Issue* in the notes to Section B. *Sugar, Bliss, More, 19, Mizz,* and *Just 17* are magazines designed specifically for the adolescent or young adult market. The others are targeted at adults.

MAGAZINES

1 This is a predicting and personalising exercise to motivate students to read the article.

Notes about the article:

The article comes from a popular magazine, founded in 1991, called *The Big Issue*. This is edited in London and sold on the streets of British cities by 'homeless, vulnerably housed and ex-homeless people' who buy the magazine at a reduced price and sell it to the public to make a slight profit. Here is part of the magazine's policy statement: *The Big Issue* 'campaigns on behalf of the homeless, highlights the major social issues of the day, gives homeless people the chance to make an income, increases the opportunity for homeless people to control their lives, allows homeless people to voice their views and opinions'. It is funded through advertising, sponsorship and sales, and its profits go to help homeless people. Similar street papers exist in Johannesburg *(Homeless Talk)* and St Petersburg *(The Depths)*.

2 Before they read the article, students familiarise themselves with some of the terms which might otherwise cause problems. They can guess first, then ask others, then consult their dictionaries. Have a class feedback before they go on to read the article.

ANSWERS

chart busters = successful pop stars
state-of-the-art = containing the latest technology
donated = given as a present
sound system (or PA) = loudspeakers, microphones and amplifiers
rationed = restricted
gig = concert
get in people's way = make life difficult for others
venue = place where concerts are held
support group = less famous band who play first at a concert
lead singer = main singer of a group
mates = close friends
producers = people in charge of a recording
curfew = time when everyone must be off the streets

3 Before going on to a second, more intensive reading, this discussion simply elicits first reactions and responses from the students. It is an opportunity for them to express their opinions about pop bands or other celebrities doing charity work. In this case the band is helping to bring normality back to a previously war-torn region, but there are many parallel cases of artists and musicians working to help other deprived or devastated regions.

4 This activity asks students to examine critically the structure and style of the article, to make inferences from the text, and finally to discuss one of its main themes.

ANSWERS

a 1, 2, 6, 7, 8, 12

b 3: the sound system, the situation in Sarajevo today; 4: the situation in Sarajevo today; 5: the feelings of two members of the band; 8, 9: the feelings of one member of the band; 10: the community music project; 11: the situation in Sarajevo today and the importance of music to it.

c Possible answers: making *The Big Issue* reporter seem closer to the band – and their report therefore more immediate, more vivid; emphasising their commitment to helping people in need rather than gaining benefits themselves.

d Possible answers: the ending is strong because it brings the reader back to the actual concert; it emphasises the common humanity of all young people, regardless of their situation; it is vivid and dramatic, contrasting light and laughter, a moment of enjoyment, with the darkness that swallows them up, a stark reminder of the recent war.

e *Dangerous*: the writer is told not to bother with seat belts – a crash is possible, and would probably be fatal; they are going to a city where water and electricity are rationed to a few hours a day; it's a recent war zone. *Badly organised in some ways*: when the band arrives, the instruments are still at the border, because they didn't have the necessary documentation; they couldn't raise money for insurance. *Well organised in some ways*: they found an indoor venue when they couldn't play outdoors; they are in a suburb relatively free of bombed-out buildings; they have a planned itinerary – Sarajevo, then Zagreb & Rimini; they have planned to leave the sound system at the university so that it can provide training for technicians and producers.

f This is a question open to personal interpretation. The article does not explain it. It is an opportunity for students to express their own views on the issue.

Further work on magazines: send off for sample copies of the UK magazines mentioned. Students can work on these as whole issues, summarising their contents and style in oral or written reports, or in the form of posters. An alternative is to ask students to prepare a presentation of the magazine they choose: this could be a press conference for the launch of the magazine, an advertisement for use on TV (an excellent 'Friday afternoon activity' to put energy back into a tired class), or any other form of dramatic presentation.

NEWSPAPERS

1 You might add the following questions: What British newspaper titles do you know? What do you know of their political alignments and affiliations?

Explore the photos of the three newspapers with the students, asking them to comment on layout, photos, headlines, the general impression given to the reader.

Notes on newspaper front pages:
'Labour keeps us …': refers to the long waiting periods for operations in the National Health Service
'Silly Billy …': a light-hearted story about a TV presenter
'Dallaglio': England rugby captain, who resigned in May 1999 after reports from a popular Sunday newspaper tricked him into a 'confession' that he had experimented with drugs as a teenager
'Botham': former England cricket star with a 'colourful' life often reported in the press
'romps': playful activities (here, of a sexual nature)

2 A comparative cultural exercise, in which students are given eleven facts about British newspapers and asked to compare with the press in their own country.

Language notes:
'political allegiance' = loyalty to a particular political party
'libel or defamation': both libel and defamation are oral and written statements which damage someone's reputation, but libel additionally implies that the statements are false.

3 Extra material, to be used as backup information, or as material for gap-filling, matching, etc.

	Millions of copies read daily	Millions sold daily
The Sun	10.1	4.0
Daily Mirror	6.5	2.5
Daily Mail	4.4	2.1
Daily Express	3.2	1.2
Daily Telegraph	2.8	1.0
Daily Star	2.0	0.8
The Times	1.7	0.8
The Guardian	1.3	0.4
The Independent	0.9	0.3
Financial Times	0.7	0.3

Source: *Social Trends* (HMSO, London); *The Guardian*

ANSWERS

a *The Guardian* is considered a 'quality' newspaper and is most likely to be thought of as more serious than the other two.   **b** a matter of personal opinion!   **c** *The Guardian* is a 'quality' newspaper; *The Express* is 'middle market'; *The Sun* is 'popular'.   **d** *The Express* 1.2 million; *The Sun* 4 m; *The Guardian* 0.4 m.

4 This is a light-hearted discussion exercise. Encourage students to think of as many reasons as possible to explain why the statements could be thought threatening.

Language notes:

'Christmas pudding' = a steamed pudding made with dried fruit, requiring quite a lot of stirring while it is being made. Here the quantities are large, so oars are referred to instead of spoons.

ANSWERS

The question about possible threats is partly a matter of personal opinion, but b, c, e and f refer to long-established British traditions, while the bizarre flavours of British crisps (g) are a more recent tradition which a visit to any pub will immediately confirm. The fishermen's hairnets are more obviously a threat to gender stereotypes rather than national traditions, but at a deeper level this touches on Britain's maritime traditions and recent controversies about foreign fleets fishing in British territorial waters.

e is true. All the rest are false.

Source of information: the European Commission in the UK, *Do you believe all you read in the papers? The Euro Myths* (London 1994)

OPTION

This activity extends the comparative aspect already started in Exercise 2. It can be done as a class project, with groups examining either different newspapers or different *aspects* of the newspapers and comparing their results. The results of their research can be presented in the form of essays, short talks, or posters.

D   BOOKS

1 Students now re-examine and discuss the section on books in the questionnaires they filled in earlier. Encourage talk about the books mentioned, and the reasons for liking them. At the end of the notes for this unit, you will find four complete British questionnaires. You can use these to give students more information and include a comparative element in this exercise.

2 ▭▭ Give students time to read and respond to the short biographical note about Roger McGough. If anyone has read other works of the poet's, they can tell the class about them. There is then a moment to read and listen to the poem (See poem on Student's Book page 66). After this, they jot down a few key ideas as a first response to the three questions before discussing them with others. The questions are deliberately phrased to encourage readers to respond personally. There is no single 'correct' reading of the poem and the important aim here is to allow a personal meaning to grow between the reader and the text.

Language notes:

'we got what it takes' (colloquial) = we are successful people (we've got what it takes to be successful)

'Eight thousand cc': the size of a car's engine is measured in cc (cubic centimetres). Small cars have 1100–1500 cc, the biggest have 7,000–7,500 cc. 'Eight thousand cc' is the total for the family's five cars.

'I run two': 'run' = use

'the missus' (colloquial) = my wife (the Mrs)

'Nippin down to Asda': 'nip down to' = go quickly. Asda is a popular supermarket chain.

'We're a load of noisy parkers': we park the car noisily, with a pun on 'nosy parker' = meddlesome, interfering person

'Carbon monoxide, Benzine dioxide' = poisonous gases in car exhaust

'Automanic': resulting from auto-mania, with a pun on 'automatic'

'dash' = style (the word also suggests speed)

'about oil ... about war' = the poem was written at the time of the Gulf War (1990)

'about time ...' = the time has come for this (automania) to end

3 [CD] This listening task is a note-taking exercise, which we have left in a simple form for the teacher to adapt according to the abilities of the class and the time available. The full interview lasts 6–7 minutes, which will be too long for most classes to take in continuously. Feel free to stop and check students' answers every 2–3 topics, or use one of these variations:

- *Jigsaw listening:* Four groups, given separate extracts from the tape and one or two topics each, make notes as they listen, then pool their results. The topics might be:
  1 Childhood and family   3 Early writings
  2 Liverpool; pop music   4 Who does he write for?

- *Listening for specific information:* Give the class some detailed questions on just one of the topics, which they can answer easily by listening. For example, on the 'early writings' topic, ask
  - How old was he when he started writing poetry?
  - Why did he start writing poetry?
  - Where did he publish his first poems?
  - What else did he publish besides poems?

- *Listen and write:* Students listen without specific questions to answer, but they are told beforehand that they will be asked to write a portrait of Roger McGough: a simple factual paragraph, or something more inventive, such as a short poem or magazine article. Students should be allowed to listen as often as they need. This is not (at first sight) an 'objective' task, but may well prove fertile in that it lets students develop their own relationships with the material – as well as helping the teacher see what they find interesting in it.

Tapescript

Unit 7D, exercise 3. An interview with Roger McGough.

I = Interviewer   RMcG = Roger McGough

RMcG   I was born in Liverpool, and grew up in Liverpool, which is a very ... when I was very young it was a major port in England. And I grew up during the War, so my very first memories as a little boy were of erm … bombs falling, and erm … searchlights and erm … it wasn't at all frightening, it was quite exciting because I was a young boy. And I enjoyed living in Liverpool with lots of relations, lots of friends, very Irish. The family – my parents' parents' parents – came from Ireland, and I think that gave me a great love of language and talking and telling stories – lots of aunties and uncles. And erm … it was a very good place to grow up in really.

I   But Liverpool came to be a very important place in the, in the culture of Britain in the nineteen sixties …

RMcG   Indeed, cause when I was very young, growing up there it declined as a large port; and people were unemployed, and it became a, a rather sad place in some ways. And, erm … and then suddenly, in the sixties, the Beatles came along and erm … there was a youth explosion, teenage, teenagers suddenly had money in their pockets erm … and Liverpool was really the focal point of a lot of the youth culture and erm … I'd been to university, I'd gone from Liverpool to Hull University and come back to be a teacher. And erm … soon I was involved in the clubs and erm … everybody there, and I even became part of a group called The Scaffold. And erm … one of the members of the group – there were three of us in it, three men – and one was called Michael McCartney – Paul McCartney's brother. And so I stopped teaching and became a sort of pop singer for a while, but only for a short while. And all the time I was then writing poetry, even The Scaffold, what we were mainly doing, as well as writing songs and singing, was doing poetry and erm … comedy … theatre, that sort of thing.

I   So is that how you became a poet, through song writing?

RMcG   Not really. It's how I got to a large audience, I think. I mean I'd started writing when I was about eighteen and I'd just left school and just gone to university and I was reading French and I suddenly became very excited about writing … about language, which I hadn't before. I'd never written poetry before that time. I'd always thought that poetry was best when it was spoken aloud. I used to enjoy reciting it when I was at school, singing the poetry, saying the poetry. I never wrote it. And I suddenly discovered when I was eighteen, seventeen or eighteen, that I really loved writing poetry. It was exciting to me, it was a way that I could express myself, in a way that I couldn't before. And so I started writing and I almost didn't show anybody at first and then I began to publish my poems in a university newspaper. And I used to draw cartoons as well, I always liked doing cartoons and drawing and painting. And … but when I came back to Liverpool, at the time of the Beatles, the sixties, that I suddenly started reading my poetry aloud to groups of people. And erm … and then because of the whole focus of people on Liverpool, the name took off and the Beatles became … and then the Liverpool poets became very famous as well. I'm not writing to please an English professor. Or a literature professor. I just write for myself and my own friends, in a way. Not consciously. I don't give them the poems but erm … it's this sort of voice that enjoys language and is surprised by it and loves it. So if I write children's poetry I don't erm … usually think today I will write a poem for children, or today I'll write an adult poem. I usually just write the poem and usually the language, an idea for language comes into it, and I start the poem. But when I've finished it, I think: 'Ah, is this a poem for children, or is it a poem for adults?' And often the editor at the erm … publisher's will decide for me. And a lot of the poems fit quite easily into each, and some poems are comic, but can be serious and some poems are children's poems and adults' poems as well. And the best are somewhere right in the middle.

4
5 A type of book that often appears in lists of this kind is the thriller. In this list, there is only 1: number 11, although 2 is also a novel of suspense. An important category in the list consists of novels about contemporary life, family histories or personal relationships: 1, 3, 5, 8, 14, 17, 18 and 20. Other kinds of books that feature are: autobiographical works: 9, 13, 16; historical novels: 2, 7, 10; works about scientific issues: 12, 15; and works that instruct or inform people about either practical issues: 6 or psychological issues: 4, 19.

6 Having seen the kinds of books that are popular in Britain, students try to think of an idea – or, if they enjoy this imaginative kind of work, they could devise a simple plot. They can join another group and compare their ideas. A follow-up would be for the class to vote for either the best or the funniest ideas – or for students to write a short synopsis of the plot or an opening scene.

APPENDIX: Complete Questionnaires

QUESTIONNAIRE

First name: Susie   Age: 16   Home town: Oxford

1 What magazines or comics do you read? The Big Issue, Q, Vox, BBC clothes show, Elle, Vogue, The Face, i-D, Select

What do you like about them? They keep you up to date on good (cheap sometimes) clothes, and music trends. Also tell you about (music) clubs and festivals.

2 What books have you had to read in the last year? Jeanette Winterson, Oranges Are Not the Only Fruit, Shakespeare, Much ado About Nothing, T. Williams, A Streetcar Named Desire, Chaucer, The Miller's Tale

What books have you chosen to read in the last year? J Gaarder, Sophie's World, E J Howard, The Beautiful Visit, F Kafka, Metamorphosis & Other Stories, Orwell, 1984, A Huxley, Brave New World & Point Counter Point, W Golding, Lord of the Flies, J Wyndham, Seeds of Time, V Woolf, Orlando, M Shelley, Frankenstein, H James, The Turn of the Screw, E Wharton, The Age of Innocence & Ethan Frome

Which ones have you liked? Write a few lines about one or two that you've particularly enjoyed.
Since reading 1984 and Brave New World I've really begun thinking, they opened my mind up to all sorts of new ideas. I found Metamorphosis really made an impression on me too, if only for the fact that it makes my skin crawl!

3 Do you read a newspaper? Which one(s)? None.

What part of the newspaper do you like best? I do read the magazine from The Observer on Sunday, it's got lots of interesting bits and bobs in it.

QUESTIONNAIRE

First name: Aideen   Age: 16   Home town: Belfast

1 What magazines or comics do you read? Sugar, Select, Big Issue

What do you like about them? I like Select best. It gives me information on music and various bands. Also, concert dates + good star signs.

2 What books have you had to read in the last year? Far From the Madding Crowd, Animal Farm, Macbeth

What books have you chosen to read in the last year? /

Which ones have you liked? Write a few lines about one or two that you've particularly enjoyed.
Animal Farm – it was animals representing the Russian Revolution, and it was very interesting and enjoyable to read.

3 Do you read a newspaper? Which one(s)? Belfast Telegraph, Sunday Life

What part of the newspaper do you like best? The star signs, day to day news.

QUESTIONNAIRE

First name: Emma   Age: 18   Home town: Belfast

1 What magazines or comics do you read? Sugar, Bliss, Eva, Woman's Own

What do you like about them? The stories

2 What books have you had to read in the last year? GNVQ Advanced Business text book

What books have you chosen to read in the last year? Diving In, X-files (Goblins)

Which ones have you liked? Write a few lines about one or two that you've particularly enjoyed.
Diving In – it was a romantic story about a 17 year old girl and all the problems that she had with the men and family in her life – it was realistic.

3 Do you read a newspaper? Which one(s)? No.

What part of the newspaper do you like best? N/A

QUESTIONNAIRE

First name: _Ariel_   Age: _16_   Home town: _London_

1 What magazines or comics do you read? _TNT Magazine_

What do you like about them? _It's free. You don't have to pay for it. It reminds me, and informs me, of my true home - Australia (that is serious!)_

2 What books have you had to read in the last year? _Kafka, The Trial_
Orwell, 1984
Dickens, Great Expectations

What books have you chosen to read in the last year? _The Black Album - Hanif Kureishi_
The Buddha of Suburbia - " "
Night Shift - Stephen King

Which ones have you liked? Write a few lines about one or two that you've particularly enjoyed.
Hanif Kureishi - very good, Asian view of London
Stephen King - just plain cool. what can I say, the man is a psychopath.

3 Do you read a newspaper? Which one(s)? _Yes, the Financial Times, The Evening Standard, The Sunday Times_

What part of the newspaper do you like best? _Garfield, and the crossword (not cryptic though!!!)_

8 HOLIDAYS

AIMS

- To explore attitudes to holidays amongst British students and invite comparative cultural evaluations
- To compare holidays in the present with those in the past
- To focus on one particular holiday activity, the picnic, stimulate personal memories and invite response to a fictional representation
- To consider local and global implications of increasing tourism in Britain and abroad

GENERAL REMARKS

Over the twentieth century, holidays have played an ever more important role in the cultural life of British people, while tourism, as in so many other countries, has become a mainstay of the economy. This unit investigates first the attitude of young people to their holidays, then compares holidays in the past and the present, and finally looks at more general issues to do with tourism and the environment.

A   SCHOOL HOLIDAYS

I It may be useful to explore the pictures with the class before beginning the exercise. The photos represent two quite different holiday experiences – the first shows a group of young men, perhaps college students or a sports team, holidaying together, enjoying a communal dip in the sea, while the other is typical of a more individual style. Encourage students to discuss the kinds of holidays that they themselves prefer. This usually provides more queries for exercise 2.

3 ▭▭ In this first listening activity, students are simply asked to check whether the British students on the tape address any of the questions that the class listed in exercise 2.

Language notes:
'save up as a family' = members of the family save their money and then use it together for their holidays
'a hell hole' (slang) = a very disagreeable place
'bizarre pockets of the world' = remote places; 'bizarre', though probably not meant seriously, does nevertheless betray the rather home-centred views of the young person speaking!

TAPESCRIPT

Unit 8A, exercise 3. Five British teenagers talk about their holidays.

I = Interviewer

I In the holidays, what do you do with your free time, do you go away and if so, would it be with the school or with some youth group or with friends or with your parents or family?

1 I don't ... Normally, we'll sort of save up as a family and go away maybe every year ... my brother's twenty-one now, so he doesn't come away with us, he just totally dislikes that. And now I've started going away less with my Mum – more with my friends. It's quite rare for me to go on holiday with my Mum now.

I And where would you go, in this country or abroad?

1 With my Mum we'd go abroad. But normally with my friends it's awful camping somewhere and it'll be a bit of a hell hole but that's part of the fun, really.

2 I tend to go away with my family ... we like America. We go there quite a lot ... various other places. But I've got a sister, very close to me in age, she's just a year older – so it's all right, going away. Now I mean, perhaps she won't come away with us so often, so I don't know what's going to happen.

3 Well, this year I went to Corfu and to Austria and both times I had friends there. And ... but once I went to Corfu with family as well, so it's a kind of bit of both, really. But I do have quite a lot of friends who live in all kinds of bizarre pockets of the world, so I go and stay with them sometimes.

4 As I mentioned, I went to Argentina with the school, so that wasn't with my parents. It all depends on finances and whether they can take time off from work as to whether we go away but normally during the holidays I'm in working with them in their office and so, you know, we don't tend to have very many trips abroad. When we do, it tends to be as a family or up to see my grandmother who lives in Cheshire.

5 I haven't been on holiday for over, well, over a year now, I mean when I did it was with family to America, France, somewhere like that. And the school doesn't often really do trips in the same way as many schools do but actually this half term we're going to Berlin ... for just four or five days and spend some time there which will be good.

Students read the nine statements before listening a second time. If your class finds the listening exercises difficult, discuss the statements with them and see which ones they agree with at this point, rather than later in exercise 5. The more familiar the vocabulary and concepts they are going to hear, the easier it will be for them to understand the recording.

ANSWERS

a   b   c   d   e   g

This serves as a round up to the theme of whether young people prefer going on holidays with others of their own age, or with parents and families. The rest of this section explores what kinds of holidays students enjoy, and what other things they do during the school's summer break.

6 A pre-listening and personalising activity. Once again, the vocabulary to be heard is seen and discussed beforehand to familiarise students with both the topic and the vocabulary.

7 📼 Students listen and tick the list in 6. You can then play the tape once more to elicit an overall response. Encourage the class to discuss the marked differences in attitudes expressed by the British students, and to compare them with their own class results from the previous exercise.

ANSWERS

Two speakers prefer holidays in cool places; three like holidaying in hot places; two like the beach; one likes being beside a pool; three like to do some tourist activities, but not too many – they like a mixture of active and lazy days.

TAPESCRIPT

Unit 8A, exercise 7. The teenagers talk about the kind of holiday they prefer.

I = *Interviewer*

I If you do go abroad on a holiday, or indeed to I don't know a seaside resort, unless you live in one, what do you most like to do? Do you like to do something active or would you rather lie on a beach?

1 I don't like the sun at all. I really can't stand it. I was born in winter. I'm just sort of designed for winter 'cause I'm so pale. I just burn so I hate lying on the beach. I like going to dark places. And cold places.

2 I'm afraid I'm the exact opposite. I spend hours and hours every day ... sprawled out on a beach. My body doesn't really agree with it, though, because I always faint ... but that's beside the point. What else ... oh no, but I mean we always ... we like going to all sorts of different places – perhaps places that most people don't go to. So obviously we do quite a bit of tourism. Sort of going round seeing the places as well.

3 Well if I go to somewhere sunny I'll do a bit of both so I'll lie ... I couldn't lie on a beach all day but equally I wouldn't want to spend, you know walk around mountains ... but all this tourism stuff gets me down after about an hour, quite honestly.

4 Well really I like to strike a balance between having ... when I go on holiday, to have a rest and then to be actually enjoying what's around you. So really I do a bit of both. Although I was born in the summer, I'm a bit like Anna, I don't particularly like the sun very much. It doesn't agree with me.

5 Yeah, I'm not into tourist type holidays. I'm keen on the beach, swimming pool, sun, that kind of thing.

8 📼 To help with the listening exercise, ask students to compare their lists before they listen to the opinions expressed on the tape.

ANSWERS

cinema, shopping, television, get a job, visit friends, help parents.

TAPESCRIPT

Unit 8A, exercise 8. The teenagers continue to talk about their holidays.

I = Interviewer

I Even if you go away with your family, presumably that's only for two or three weeks. What do you do with the rest of your long school summer holiday?

5 Well, there's very little to do, to be honest. I mean … It's the standard free time and entertainment, sort of … thing, cinema, shops, sort of thing we've talked about I suppose … and television. A lot.

I You've talked about working with your parents during the holidays.

4 That's right. I get drafted in, normally it's sort of reception, computer duties, that sort of thing; and that tends to be 9 till 5 Mondays to Fridays, so the weekends tend to be the free time, then it's, you know, shopping or whatever.

3 When I'm in Bristol, it depends a lot whether people are around. You know obviously, if friends are elsewhere then, there's not much to do. My Dad lives in London so I normally spend a few days with him, here and there and again I have friends who live in south London, but because he lives in north London, it takes longer to get to south London from north London than from Bristol. So that's useful.

2 I sleep and I eat and I sometimes get some jobs. I was working at a solicitor's and a stockbroker's and places like that really.

I I got a job last holiday which was OK but I'm not really used to it. I mean, I got the money but then I spent the money. I generally like sort of going off for the day to different places and my friends will suddenly go 'Ah, I know! Let's go to Brighton.' And we'll just disappear for a bit. And that's what I like doing. But I don't generally go away on sort of a set holiday, I won't plan anything. Just … things happen.

9 After a lot of listening and personal exchanges, a low-key vocabulary exercise rounds off this section.

ANSWERS

to go – away, on holiday, to Berlin, with my parents, and stay with friends, to see my grandmother, to dark places

to do – trips abroad, quite a bit of tourism, something active, a bit of both

---

Preparation for the next section. Students are asked do some personal research before they go on to the next part, which focuses on a comparison between holidays in the past and the present. Some students may not be able to question their own parents or grandparents – emphasise that they can interview any older person they know. The scene can be set for the class by a brainstorming exercise – students predict some of the main themes that may emerge from their enquiries, and list them on the board. The information they then gather is to be presented to the class as feedback in the first exercise of section B.

B PAST AND PRESENT

1 The information presented can lead to a more extended project on the differences between holidays past and present. Students could collect family photos or reproductions of paintings for a poster exhibition. Diaries from their own relatives or extracts from novels can also be used to build up a picture of past holidays in their country.

2 The 'game' element in this activity helps students to focus more closely on the different images on the page, which show different types of holidays in the nineteenth (the painting, top left) and early twentieth century. Donkey rides used to be a popular feature of the British seaside. There are more detailed notes on the pictures in 3 below.

3 Students interpret the photos to produce a simple comparison between holidays now and holidays in the past.

ANSWERS

Details which could be added to the 'Holidays in the past' section of the grid, from the pictures on p. 70, include:

Destination: the seaside; the countryside for camping holidays

Holiday clothes: the nineteenth-century painting shows women fully clothed in long dresses and hats, while the man wears a bathing costume and a hat. The early twentieth-century photos show: children riding donkeys in quite formal suits and hats; women and children camping in dresses, aprons, jumpers, etc. – clothes that would not be different from their everyday wear; and, in the bottom right picture, people strolling along the beach in their everyday clothes, with one man in bathing trunks, while his companion has simply rolled up his trouser legs to wade in the sea.

Holiday activities: the three people in the foreground of the painting are chatting, reading, or doing needlework, while some others splash in the sea behind them; photos: donkey riding for children, filling mattresses with straw, strolling or sailing toy boats.

4 In this exercise, students are asked to interpret two graphs. The first one shows that the number of holidays taken by British people has been rising since 1967 – more people are taking either two or three holidays per year – while the number of people who either take no holidays at all, or only one holiday per year, has been falling slightly. The second compares the number of British people who holiday in Britain with the number who go abroad; the former has remained fairly stable since the 1960s, while the latter has risen quite sharply. If it is useful for your class, you could give them the following supplementary information about recent holiday patterns in Britain (from *Social Trends* 1999).

• Twenty per cent of holidays taken in the United Kingdom have an activity as their main purpose, with the most popular being hill walking, rambling (usually = organised walks in groups) or orienteering (an organised walk in which participants are given some clues and have to find their way by map-reading).

- The most popular holiday destinations in Britain, at the end of the twentieth century, were the West Country (England) where about a fifth of holiday makers converged, followed by Scotland and Wales.
- The most popular holiday destination for Britons travelling abroad was Spain – over a quarter of holidays abroad were in that country. The popularity of France and the USA also increased, with the USA the most popular destination outside Europe, and the third overall.

5 **6** 5 and 6 are round-up exercises, in which students review the information they have gained from part B and from the British students interviewed in A, as well as their own knowledge of present-day holiday patterns. In exercise 6 they are asked to assess the changes that have occurred. People take more holidays now than in the past, but are they necessarily better, healthier, more enjoyable? Encourage brainstorming – reasons given can be listed on the board.

C PICNICS

1 A warm-up to the theme of picnics. This exercise often works well as a whole class guided fantasy. Ask the class to shut their eyes (if this is something they are willing to do!) and try to imagine themselves at a childhood picnic. In their minds, they recreate the scene: how it felt and looked, where it was, who was with them, etc. Ask them to consider the questions in turn, e.g. where they went, and to write down a few notes. Afterwards, they use their notes to describe their remembered picnic to a partner. You can round off the activity by asking listeners to report to the class on any unusual or interesting things they heard when their partners described the picnics.

2 The picture represents a picnic in the nineteenth century, and is full of activity of all sorts. The role play asks students to imagine that they are actually taking part in the picnic, and is a way of getting them to look more closely at all the characters and activities represented. It carries forward the theme of the differences between holidays in the past and present.

3 Roddy Doyle is an Irish writer, so strictly speaking this is not a 'British' picnic – although it very easily could be. This poignant fictional depiction of a modern outing is in many senses the opposite of the bucolic, romantic, happy experience portrayed in the picture students have just been exploring. The activities suggested are creative ones, intended to help students understand the atmosphere of the piece. Retelling the story from the point of view of the mother, who is obviously struggling to maintain family peace, and the father, who is irritated and sullen, will sharpen the sense that students have of the two characters. After this initial 'gist' exercise, students are invited, as in Unit 5, to respond to a literary extract through drama. Dramatising a scene takes it out of the print medium into the three-dimensional world, and it often allows students to express their reactions and emotions in a 'physical' way that many students find easier or more effective – certainly more memorable – than simply speaking or writing about them.

Notes about the writer:

Roddy Doyle was born in Dublin in 1958, and taught English in a community school in north Dublin. His first novel, *The Commitments*, was very well received when it was published in 1988, and shortly afterwards became even more widely known when it was made into a film by Alan Parker. It is the first in a series of three novels, known as the Barrytown trilogy, which have all been made into successful films. The later novel, *Paddy Clarke, Ha Ha Ha*, won the prestigious Booker prize award in 1993. It is narrated by a 10-year-old boy, Paddy Clarke, who lives in Dublin. In the extract, his father and mother take him, his younger brother Sinbad and their baby sister Catherine out for a picnic. Everything goes wrong – it's raining, the family have to stay in the car, the father insists that they eat the picnic there instead of going back home. His bad temper and the barely suppressed conflict between the two parents make the outing a very uncomfortable one for the family.

Language notes:

The narrator's name, Patrick, is a very common one in Ireland, so much so that the nickname associated with it, Paddy, is often used as a synonym for an Irishman.

'Da' = a child's name for Daddy, father in Ireland; it is slightly marked for class, indicating that the family come from a background that is not very wealthy

'Cortina' = the brand name of a small car

'bloody eejit' (Irish slang) = idiot; the father scolds Paddy for continuing to nag about going to the mountains – he uses the swear word 'bloody' coupled with 'eejit'

'Jesus Christ!': once again, the father swears, this time at his younger son for wanting to get out to go to the toilet, and the mother remonstrates with him for it: her saying 'Pat', the father's name, is an appeal for him to stop

'dished out the picnic' = gave it to the boys

'Fanta' = a tinned soft drink, orange-flavoured

D   HOLIDAYS AND TOURISM

1 It may be best to set this exercise as homework before the class starts this part. Students could research the most visited places in the local public library, the tourist bureau, travel agencies, or the Internet. In class, list the tourist sites on the board. Elicit views on the places from students who have been to them.

2
3 Exercises 2 and 3 move from the particular to the more general. First students think of positive or negative effects of tourists in their own country, then of tourism more generally. This familiarises students with the issues that they are going to encounter in the information given about Britain, and sets the scene for the cross-cultural comparisons they are asked to make in subsequent exercises. Students exchange views in pairs or small groups before reporting to the class.

4 This should be a light-hearted guessing game. Students may know some of the places listed, for example the Tower of London and St Paul's Cathedral. For others, there are clues in the photos – for example the Palace Pier, Brighton, or the historical figures in the wax museum.

76

> **ANSWERS**
>
> a 4   b 9   c 5   d 3   e 2   f 8   g 10   h 1   i 6   j 7

5 Encourage students to describe not just the tourist sites, but their feelings as they visited. To prepare for the next activities, ask them to try to remember how many visitors were there with them, and whether they felt the sites were too crowded. If most students haven't visited any of the places, ask them to look carefully at the photos and imagine the experience of being there. Ask them to choose their favourite spot to visit, if they had one choice only, and compare it with others.

6 This is an authentic article from a newspaper and it may present some vocabulary difficulties. As usual, students are asked to read quickly for gist, and not worry too much in the first reading if there is anything they don't understand. You can then invite them to report one difficulty to the class: Does anyone else in the class know that particular word or expression? If not, ask them to try to guess the meaning from the context.

Language notes:
'heritage' = anything precious handed down to new generations
'inundation' = literally, a flood; metaphorically a very great quantity, overwhelming numbers
'tarmac' = the material that roads and airport runways are made of
'the mighty tide' (metaphorical expression) = overwhelming numbers
'under the press of' = caused by the pressure of
'the jams of people' = crowds so dense that they stop or restrict movement
'progressive closing down of sensitive sites' = overcrowded sites gradually being closed down
'mythic and improbable' = so unlikely that they seem to be fictional
'cherished places' = places that are greatly loved
'take its course unimpeded' = to carry on without any restrictions
'allowing loggers to have their way in Amazonia': refers to the controversy surrounding the cutting down of rainforests in South America
'an optimum number' = the greatest number possible
'time ticketing' = the act of restricting the number of tourists who are allowed to visit a site at any one time, and also the time that they can spend there.

7 Students extract the article's opinions first. Then they discuss them and compare them with their own opinions about their country's tourist industry.

> **ANSWERS**
>
> 1, 2, 3, 4, 7

8 The last exercise is an optional one for classes which enjoy debates. This can be set up as described in the Teacher's Notes for Unit 3A, exercise 7: Organising a mini-debate.

UNIT 9

NATURE AND THE ENVIRONMENT

AIMS

- To give an idea of the physical geography of Britain and the language used to describe it
- To consider the connections between the weather and British culture
- To provide historical and contemporary perspectives on British attitudes to nature
- To introduce students to British environmental issues and organisations, and the way they are presented to the public
- To invite cross-cultural comparisons

GENERAL REMARKS

The relationship of humanity to the natural world is often seen as a global issue, with international organisations giving warnings about the worldwide consequences of the greenhouse effect, the melting polar ice cap, El Niño, the destruction of rainforests, etc. These are vital concerns, of course. Yet the habit of thinking globally needs to be complemented by an understanding of local conditions and cultures. These differ greatly from one country to another. Even within Britain there are important differences – amounting to contradictions – between regions, communities and individuals in their attitudes to the environment.

The building of new houses, supermarkets, roads, railways and airports, whether fox-hunting should be banned, whether farmers should be allowed to grow genetically modified crops – these are issues of urgent public concern, exhaustively discussed in parliament, on radio and TV and in the newspapers. Perhaps the greatest tension in Britain, however, is between the needs of urban and rural populations. A majority of the population has been living in cities in Britain since the mid-19th century, yet many of those who live in cities have a nostalgic desire to be in contact with nature – while many people who live in the country are keen to have urban-style facilities. There are ironies and complexities everywhere you look.

Our approach in this unit has been to look first at the realities of Britain's natural environment – its physical geography, its weather – then at people's attitudes to nature, and finally at environmental issues today.

A THE PHYSICAL ENVIRONMENT

1 The point of this exercise is to establish a basis for thinking about the geography of Britain. Students start on familiar ground, describing their own country, and should be able to move on from there with increased confidence. It may help to have a large map of your country on the wall as a visual aid.

This is also an opportunity to revise or teach the appropriate items of vocabulary, many of which will come up again in the following exercises.

2 The inadequacy of maps as representations of reality becomes evident in an exercise such as this. At this stage of the unit, keep things simple. It is enough for students to make observations such as 'Britain is a collection of islands' or 'The main rivers of Scotland are the Clyde, the Dee, the Spey, the Don and the Tay'. Any supplementary material you or your students can bring to class – slides, holiday photos, travel brochures, detailed maps – will contribute greatly.

A possible alternative is to do exercise 3 first, and then, with the extra knowledge gained, do exercise 2.

3 After a brief vocabulary check, students are asked to gather and compare information from two types of sources, written and photographic. They will have to look at both quite carefully, and think about the meanings of the words with some precision. (The difference between chalk and granite is crucial, for instance.) Note that from the evidence of the texts the third picture (of chalk cliffs) could be Flamborough, Dover or the Seven Sisters. In fact it is Dover, but students who choose any of the others would not, in the terms of this exercise, be wrong.

Language notes:
'layer cake' = a cake with two or more layers, with jam or cream in between.

ANSWERS

(*From the top*) granite cliffs in Cornwall; salt marshes in East Anglia; the White Cliffs of Dover (but could also be Flamborough or the Seven Sisters); a sea loch in north-west Scotland.

4 This is a chance for students to react imaginatively to the pictures on this page. As well as offering an escape from the technical language of the geographer, this will help to prepare them for the personal responses to nature which they will encounter in part C.

B THE WEATHER

1 Selecting the most important facts for a visitor is, of course, an indirect way of helping students absorb these facts themselves. Of the ten facts presented, students could choose three or five, working individually; then compare with a partner.

Before your class reads the facts, you could present some of them as a dictation, which students can then check against the book. Alternatively, give students a gapped dictation of some facts; they guess possible completions, then check with the book.

ANSWERS

Possible answers to the first two questions:

Practical advice should definitely include a warning that visitors must be prepared for rapid changes of temperature; that people in search of sunshine and warmth should go to the south coast; that they should be prepared for rain (there is no dry season). In summer, visitors should have rainproof clothes and umbrellas, light clothes and hats for possible sunshine, and some warm clothes, sweaters and jackets for example, for changing temperatures; in winter, warm clothes (coats, scarves and jackets) are advisable, and rain wear is a must.

2 ▭▭ Listening for gist: students need only write down the essentials of this radio weather forecast, as indicated in the answers box. It may be worth checking first that they can locate the places mentioned. You could also play it in sections if they find it hard to understand. Note that the forecast does not give details for Northern Ireland and Scotland tomorrow, so the final box should be blank.

ANSWERS

The weather forecast confirms many of the facts listed in Exercise 1, but not **d**, **e** or **i**.

Place	Today	Tonight	Tomorrow
East Anglia, Lincolnshire, North East England	cloud light rain cold wind 4–5	frost East Anglia (0 to ⁻1 degrees) NE England 0 to ⁻3 degrees	mist & fog
North West England, Midlands, Wales, Southern England	dry, sunny cloud on S coast strong winds easing 4–5 degrees	frost inland ⁻3 or ⁻4 degrees	freezing fog patches
Northern Ireland, Scotland	dry, some sun temperatures rising; mild in NW Scotland 6 degrees. further south 3 or 4, Glasgow 5	cloud, rain, sleet in N Scotland; elsewhere: clear & frosty; freezing fog Stornaway 5 degrees, S Scotland ⁻2, N Ireland ⁻3	

TAPESCRIPT

Unit 9B, exercise 2. A weather forecast.

And now the detailed forecast for the next twenty-four hours, starting with East Anglia, Lincolnshire, and the North East of England. A gentle flow of air from the North Sea is bringing cloud and a few spots of light rain, but this will tend to thin and break, the showers dying out later this afternoon. The wind is rather cold, so the temperature won't get much above four or five degrees today. Tonight there'll be a frost, with temperatures dropping to zero or minus one in East Anglia, as low as minus two or minus three in North East England. Parts of Lincolnshire and North East England may see a few mist and fog patches by dawn tomorrow morning. Now to the Midlands, Wales, North West England, and all of Southern England, where there's likely to be a pretty dry afternoon. There are some bands of cloud circulating, especially along the south coasts from Dorset to Cornwall, but apart from that it's fine, with some pleasant sunshine on the west coast of Wales and parts of the Midlands. Strong north-easterly winds, especially in the English Channel, will slowly ease this afternoon, though temperatures will remain around four or five. Tonight, with little wind, it'll be frosty, especially away from the coast, temperatures falling as low as minus three or minus four. In parts of the Midlands, Wales and North West England there may be a few freezing fog patches to start the day tomorrow. So that's England and Wales. Now to Northern Ireland and Scotland. It's going to be a dry day here as well, slowly warming up over the afternoon, with some really quite pleasant winter sunshine. At the moment it's sunny in Aberdeen, Glasgow and Belfast. For the Northern Isles it's a different story. There's a weather front approaching Shetland and Orkney, and that will bring rain or showers by the end of the afternoon. In the North West of Scotland, south-westerly winds are bringing milder air, so temperatures here around six Celsius. Further south only three or four degrees over much of Scotland, and five for Belfast. Tonight we can expect cloud and patchy rain, some sleet perhaps, to edge into the north of mainland Scotland. Otherwise it'll be clear and frosty, with some freezing fog. Lowest temperatures: five for Stornoway, but minus two in the Borders of Scotland and minus three in Northern Ireland.

3 These opinions are all of course personal theories; after students have identified the correct summaries, you could ask them to decide which they agree with, if any. They should also feel welcome to contribute their own ideas.

ANSWERS
a 1   b 3   c 5   d 4

4 A puzzle which recycles some of the vocabulary from the weather forecast.

ANSWERS
1 fine   2 fog   3 temperature   4 clear   5 cloud   6 wind   7 degrees   8 sunshine 9 frost   10 mild   11 freezing   12 cold   13 dry   14 showers   15 mist

C ATTITUDES TO NATURE

This personalising exercise, together with the listening that follows, raises one of the most absorbing questions in the art of translation: What ideas does a word suggest in the mind of a native speaker? It is important, therefore, to allow students to reflect on their word for 'nature' in all its ramifications – without inhibition or fear of getting it wrong. As this is a personal matter, it is best done individually. Feedback can be in pairs or small groups. By recording their ideas in the tree diagram, students will have a means of making detailed comparisons with the speakers on the tape and the extracts in the following exercises. At the end of this section, as a revision exercise, students could make a second tree diagram for the word 'nature' in English.

2
3
 The same interview is played twice here: once for exercise 2 (writing down key words), and once for exercise 3. You can of course play the interview more than twice if you think it necessary.

ANSWERS

Richard: control, observe, quiet.
Alex: friendly, dangerous.
Richard: quiet, dangerous.
Wendy: grass, sky, animals, man.
Alex: pleasant.
Wendy: needed, artificial.

TAPESCRIPT

Unit 9C, exercise 2. Three English people talk about nature.

R = Richard   A = Alex   W = Wendy

R   Nature is basically those things in the world that man doesn't control, that he can with privilege observe from time to time, from afar or close, by being quiet; but they are those things that carry on regardless of him.

A   Do you think of nature as something friendly, or something violent and dangerous?

R   I think of it as quiet and friendly, but of course it can be violent and dangerous to man, such as the sea, which can be both of those things, and often is.

A   Wendy, what associations does the word nature have for you?

W   Nature to me is grass and flowers and sky and birds, and animals, but for me to a lesser degree animals, and an area of countryside which man has not ruined.

A   So it's something very pleasant, something restorative?

W   Oh very definitely so. And something which is needed by man as a contrast to the artificial world in which most of us spend our working life now.

4 🔁 After the detailed gap-filling of the previous exercise, students may need to be reminded that the point here is to get the gist, the main point, of what is said. Alternatively, as a break from listening, they could do exercise 6 here, or begin work on an English version of the word-tree. It is interesting to note that both Richard and Wendy enjoy nature in a rather energetic way, and take pleasure both in its tranquility and its drama.

ANSWERS

Richard: going into woods at dusk and watching animals, or standing on the coast (at Lyme Regis) watching a storm.

Wendy: going somewhere away from villages and cars; walking and climbing mountains in the Hebrides; watching clouds 'racing in from the Atlantic'.

TAPESCRIPT

Unit 9C, exercise 4. Richard and Wendy describe how they get close to nature.

A = Alex   R = Richard   W = Wendy

A   So if you want to go and get close to nature, how do you do it?

R   In recent times my favourite occupation has been to go walking in woods at dusk to watch for animals at that time which appear furtively, which don't appear during the day; and the most exciting thing is to see a movement among some dusky undergrowth, and see a deer coming or standing, or seeing a fox taking its prey across the field. That's very exciting and something we have to wait and watch for. We don't control this. We just observe and learn and respect.

A   What about you, Wendy? Where do you go to get close to nature?

W   Well, it's become very difficult these days. One has to often take a map, look where there are very few villages, where the roads are very small, and where you can go where you do not hear the sound of the motor car.

A   And where would you go in the British Isles to find a natural environment?

R   I was imagining standing on a man-made object, which is the Cobb at Lyme Regis, being surrounded by a storm. So to go to the coast and watch the awful power of the sea, and the sky moving fast overhead, something we have certainly no control of, would be very dramatic, very dramatic.

A   And what about outside England? I mean there's all of Scotland and Ireland and Wales. If you could go anywhere, if you had let's say a week, where would you go in the British Isles, Wendy?

W   I think the part of the British Isles that's given me the most happiness in the last few years that I've been to are the islands off Scotland. They're all very very different. They're all ... still contain people who are pursuing the crafts they have done for a long time, and I remember with particular joy the Outer Hebrides and particularly the island of Harris, which has the most incredible undulating landscape, with lots of water. And climbing the highest mountain on Harris, which is Clisham, and standing on a ridge with the clouds racing in from the Atlantic was probably the most exhilarating experience I've had for a long time.

5 ◘◘ Here the two speakers explain how they see themselves and their attitudes to nature in the context of society as a whole. (If it helps to 'place' them socially, Richard and Wendy are an educated middle-class couple, aged around 55. He is an engineer, she is a science teacher.)

ANSWERS

They feel their attitude is unusual, because most people, especially younger people, are more interested in shopping and are unwilling to make the effort to go out and make contact with nature.

TAPESCRIPT

Unit 9C, exercise 5. Other people's attitudes to nature.

A = Alex   R = Richard   W = Wendy

A   Do you think your attitudes to nature are fairly common in Britain today, or would you say that they are unusual?

R   I think a lot of people are trapped in the materialist way of life, and dominated especially, and manipulated by the television, and don't get out and appreciate nature as much as they could. So they're diverted from some pleasures which they could have. So I consider involving yourself with nature means a little effort, and a lot of people don't make that effort, they're diverted by other things. So I think we're probably in a minority.

W   I'd agree. I'd agree. I think it's also to do with generations. We're older now, and we have done some of the other things, and we understand now that going back to the basics, going back to see countryside, fresh air, actually do give us more pleasure than an afternoon shopping. But I'm afraid that we are in the minority – maybe not in the minority in our own generation, but among the other generations, the younger generation – I feel particularly now that the younger generation are not taking as much exercise, but maybe this is a pleasure they will find in the future.

6 This exercise requires a mixture of personal and cross-cultural responses, and should stimulate a good variety of opinion. As for the 'Britishness' of the texts, it may be noticed that 2, 3 and 4 reflect a number of points made by the speakers on the recording (about the restorative power of nature, and the destructive influence of man). The quote from Oscar Wilde is typical of his taste for paradox and witty contradiction of commonly held ideas. His view might reasonably be held to be typically British in its individualism and eccentricity.

Language notes:
Text 3: 'like stair-rods' = so hard it was like the iron rods which hold carpets in place on stairs.
Text 4: 'e'er' = ever
'thee/thy' (no longer used except in dialect) = you/your

D ENVIRONMENTAL ISSUES TODAY

1 Although students are asked simply to choose one organisation, they should also be ready to explain their choice to a partner or a small group – or possibly in writing.

Language notes:
National Trust: 'scheduled ancient monuments' = officially classified monuments
Ramblers: 'lobbying' = persuading influential people in the government
'pressure group' = a group dedicated to lobbying or influencing public opinion
'watchdog activities' = checking that public rights are maintained

2 This is a reflective exercise in which students are asked to analyse the means by which they were persuaded to make a choice. The point of the activity is partly to develop awareness of methods of persuasion, but also to make the student look more carefully and objectively at the texts.

ANSWERS

Statistics are used most by the National Trust ('some 240,000 hectares', 'over 300 historic houses', etc.); also 'song thrush ... numbers on farmland have dropped by 73%' (RSPB).

Financial benefits and gifts are listed at the end of each statement. Examples: 'free admission to all National Trust properties', 'discounts in outdoor equipment shops' (Ramblers), 'free bird table' (RSPB).

History/national pride: 'historic houses and gardens', 'ancient monuments', 'industrial monuments', 'our heritage' (NT).

Readers' emotions: 'our countryside', 'beautiful countryside and unspoilt coastline', 'these wonderful places' (NT); 'a national footpath network, the mosaic of national parks' (Ramblers); 'the beautiful wild birds of our countryside', 'everyone loves the song thrush', 'our gardens and the countryside' (RSPB).

Social responsibility: 'protecting ... for the lasting enjoyment of everyone', 'as a charity dependent on public support, the Trust relies on membership subscriptions', 'cares for ... unspoilt coastline ... villages ... Sites of Special Scientific Interest ... national nature reserves ... protects all these places for ever' etc. (NT); 'a recreation chosen by a quarter of the population', 'the freedom of us all' (Ramblers); 'needs more members so we can protect more birds under threat', 'many other birds ... are showing serious decline', 'with your support it could all be very different' (RSPB).

Good value for money: 'A membership fee is a small price to pay for the lasting protection of these wonderful places' (NT); 'the subscription is a small price to pay to enhance the freedom of us all' (Ramblers).

4 An opportunity to apply some of the persuasive techniques analysed in the previous exercises. Students may well enjoy the chance to read each other's efforts, perhaps in a wall display.

Further work: If your class is particularly interested in nature and the natural or man-built environment, you may like to look at Lawrence Raw, *The Country and the City*, British Council 1997.

BEING YOUNG TODAY

- To give information about the lifestyles and concerns of young people in Britain
- To re-examine stereotypes about youth culture
- To explore and discuss how youth is represented by the media and by creative writers
- To invite comparative cultural discussion

GENERAL REMARKS

The last fifty years have seen 'youth culture' attaining increasing prominence in British media reports and the analyses of social historians. The hordes of teenagers surrounding the Beatles in the Sixties and the advent of 'flower power' children advocating alternative lifestyles heralded a new era in which young people became initiators of cultural patterns, not just passive consumers. Over the next two decades, clashes between rival gangs of youths, the 'mods' and 'rockers', motorbike rallies that alarmed quiet seaside towns, the often startling hairdos and clothing of the 'punk' generation – all these were often portrayed by the media as indications of rebellious youth's threatening powers. In the Nineties, the children of the Sixties suddenly found themselves parents of a generation as eager as they had been to distinguish themselves from the society created by their elders. However, for the new 'rave generation' (a term referring to all-night parties at usually secret locations) rebelliousness now seemed overshadowed with darker threats of drugs, disease, and increasing social alienation. In addition, young people with more disposable income than ever before were conscious of being targeted by commercial interests as well as by the media, always on the lookout for scandal and sensation. But how close in fact are the headlines to the actual lives of most young people today? In this book, we have often tried to allow young people to have their say about the various cultural issues explored. Now we let them tell us about their real, everyday lives.

A   LIFESTYLES

1   Students fill in the questionnaire for their own country first. It is sometimes surprising how little people from the same country can agree on some of these facts, and this can often lead to general discussion in the class. When students begin to guess about Britain, they should take into account the clue (to number 8 in the questionnaire) provided in the three photos, which show young people doing part-time jobs in shops, restaurants, or outdoor markets.

2 An information-gap activity. The two groups should work independently of each other and not show each other their texts. Tell students that they will find some but not all of the answers for Britain in their articles. Encourage them to scan the texts quickly to find specific answers to the ten questions. They should not worry too much about detailed comprehension for the moment – the two exercises which follow are designed to help with specific vocabulary difficulties.

3 An oral feedback exercise. When students are ready, ask them to put aside the texts of the articles. Each one meets a student who has read the other text. Together, they work through the questions, giving each other the answers they found in their texts and writing down the ones given to them by their partner.

ANSWERS

1 yes   2 yes   3 no   4 yes   5 yes   6 yes   7 yes   8 no (only one quarter)   9 yes   10 yes

---

4
5 These are more intensive exercises which ask students to re-read both texts closely and work out the meanings of expressions which they may not know, from the context.

ANSWERS

Exercise 4
1e   2h   3j   4i   5d   6a   7c   8f   9b   10g

Exercise 5
a pocket money   **b** computer-literate   **c** source of income   **d** put into perspective
e consumer durables   **f** childless homes   **g** pastime

---

6 Having found specific answers in their texts and worked more intensively with the vocabulary, students are now asked to consider the facts conveyed by the two texts, and to compare these with the situation in their own countries. The two texts, and particularly Text A, challenge negative media stereotypes about young people. Contrary to the impressions that can be left by reports of 'decadent youths who terrorise their seniors', recent surveys show that the majority of young people lead quite 'virtuous' lives, although they also point to the rising importance in their lifestyles of money and television.

Students start by looking again at the questionnaire in Exercise 1, to find out what are the most significant differences (if any) between young people in their country and in Britain, then they are asked to give their own impressions of the facts they have encountered.

7 Ask students to read the three short extracts through. If necessary, discuss any language problems with them. Invite them to try to find the meanings of words or expressions they don't know from the context. They can then join a partner or a small group to discuss the articles and to think about headlines. Ask them to write their headlines on the board for easy comparison.

Language notes:

'lucrative' = something that produces a profit (in this case the fact that children have pocket money is seen by companies as a situation from which they can profit)

'leisure goods' = any product used for pastimes or free-time activities – sports equipment, music centres, cassettes, CDs, magazines, etc.

'help earn their keep' = have a part-time job to add to their spending power, so that parents do not have to give them as much pocket money

'TSB' = the name of the British bank that conducted the survey of spending patterns

8 A listing and discussion activity which invites cross-cultural comparison and comment.

B   ISSUES

1 The texts in the previous section mentioned that young people today are more likely to be 'green' than their parents. But is that true of all of them? What do young people really care about today? This section starts off by a brainstorming exercise, which asks students to give their own answers and opinions, before they listen to what their British counterparts said when asked the same question. Issues are written on the board as a visual checklist to help with the listening exercise later.

2   ▭ The five photos on the page give some clues to the issues identified in the interviews students are going to hear. Explore them with the class as a pre-listening warm-up. They show, clockwise from top left, homelessness (there are now many young people living 'rough' on the streets in Britain); politics (young people interviewed tended to be cynical about the motives and effectiveness of politicians); helping to clean up the environment; a protest against genetically modified foods; and two friends totally absorbed in the computer (many older people envy the ease with which the younger generation can enter into new technologies).

This listening is quite a long one, but is split into two parts, the first focusing on interviews in England, the second in Scotland. It will probably be easier for the class if you stop the recording after the first part and deal with that before going on to the second. If your students find listening difficult, go over possible issues with them beforehand, using the list on the board from Exercise 1; encourage them simply to listen for key words and pick those out. You can then play the recording a second time and let them add any other ideas they missed the first time round.

ANSWERS

Issues mentioned: Aids, underage pregnancy, drugs; homelessness; the environment; getting a student grant and getting to university; money problems; the weather

All the students seemed sceptical of politicians and party politics, though the last interviewed did stress that he wouldn't say he had no interest in politics.

TAPESCRIPT

Unit 10B, exercise 2. Students in England and Scotland talk about the main issues that interest young people today. The recording is in two parts.

Unit 10B, exercise 2. Part 1. English students talk about the main issues of interest to them today.

I = *Interviewer*

 I What do you think are the main issues young people are interested in today in Britain?

 1 I think that young people today aren't interested at all in interests like politics. I mean, you know, none of my friends will spend hours and hours discussing new political things. I don't know … main issues. Things like AIDS, under-age pregnancy, I mean they're just sort of predominant issues, seem to crop up everywhere … drugs, things like that.

 2 I don't think many people my age are that interested in politics, I mean, I think they're all as bad as each other. They'd all sell their own grandmothers to get into power, so I'm deeply sceptical of them all. I'm very interested in problems like homelessness. I work at a homeless shelter in the holidays. I think especially around Christmas that's so important. It's really easy, especially in a place like Clifton, to forget how other people are living. But I think again, as Sophie was saying, it's issues that affect us … sort of under-age pregnancy type things, and drugs.

Unit 10B, exercise 2. Part 2. Scottish students were asked the same question.

 I Are there any issues that you're interested in or that you think people of your age are interested in?

 1 There's lots of different issues. I think the environment is quite an important one. Just you know you get your student grants and so on. People are worried they're not going to get into Uni. Money problems, like that.

 I Any issues of particular interest to you?

 2 No, not really, just the weather. I don't know, it just disgusts me. I can't live in this climate. I want to move to a nice sunny place.

 I Such as …?

 2 I don't know, Ibiza, or something. Somewhere nice and sunny with decent night life. I don't know. A lot more beaches.

 I How about you?

 3 Issues that affect me …

 I Or that you're interested in …

 3 I suppose there's the legalisation of drugs and things. A lot of young people seem very interested in that. They were something like the second most voted for party by young men in the last election. It doesn't really affect me in a major way, I'm not a drug dealer or anything, but I can't really see what justification there is for having them – drugs – illegal.

 I Are any of you interested in politics in the sense of party politics and if so do you support a particular political party? Anybody?

 4 I certainly have political views, but not in the sense of the parties, I believe they're all pretty much the same. They're all capitalist parties supporting the same sort of agenda, doing the same sort of things, just in slightly different ways, with slightly different emphases. So I don't support any particular party but I wouldn't say I have no interest in politics, though.

3 A debate on one of the issues that have come up in the preceding activities. Choose one that students have identified in their own country. See notes to Unit 3A, exercise 7 for ways of organising the debate.

4 A personalising exercise, to set the scene for the next listening task.

5 ◖◗ Quite a long listening, but students listen for gist only, and to compare with their own opinions. If your students find listening difficult, write the interviewer's two questions on the board:

1 Anything you dread about your future? Do you think the world's going to blow itself up?
2 What do you anticipate with most pleasure?

Discuss the questions with the class, ask for predictions, and write them on the board. If you feel your students need even more help – ask them to write two columns in their notebook:

Greatest fears   What they look forward to

Then dictate some of the key words they are going to hear on the recording. Discuss any that may not be familiar. Students write them down in what they judge to be the appropriate column. They compare notes with each other and check whether they've all chosen the same categories.

Key words: a nice house, a decent job, a fairer society, overpopulation, booming world population, World War Three, complete collapse of all economies, famine and wars, unemployment, computers.

Play the recording in parts, once or twice – students tick similarities with their answers on the board, or with the key words they wrote in the notebooks.

After listening, students talk about anything they found interesting in what the British students said. Do they particularly agree with anything they heard? Do they feel that on the whole the young people on the recording are radicals, eager to change the world, or fairly conservative? How does that compare with attitudes in their own class?

TAPESCRIPT
Unit 10B, Exercise 5. English and Scottish students talk about their hopes and fears for the future.

I = *Interviewer*

I Anything you dread about your future … the future? Do you think the world's going to blow itself up?

I No, no, no. I just I'd just like to go into a job that I really enjoy. And hopefully, just all the usual things – have a nice house, maybe some kids, I'm not too sure, but I'd just like a nice, like solid, easy future, with a decent job.

2 Worries abut the future? I just hope that everything goes OK for me and there hasn't been a World War III by then or a complete collapse of all economies, or whatever. So long as things don't change too … I think a fairer society would be quite a good thing to have by then, but it would take a lot of time and effort for that to happen. I don't know if that's going to happen within my lifetime.

1   What's your greatest fear about the future, and what do you anticipate with most pleasure in the future?

3   I don't think I've really got any fears about the future. I mean, at all, really, I mean, I'm pretty confident about everything in general. Just sort of things will keep … technological change is so great now, you know we're looking at Utopia by next week.

1   And what do you look forward to with the greatest pleasure?

3   Greatest pleasure … I don't know, I mean I think I don't sort of see any particular pleasure in the future … I mean things staying exactly as they are would be fine for me.

4   I think the greatest fear I have is a booming world population. I think estimates of 10 billion by the year 2080 are rather conservative and I think if we actually get anything above that then I think there'll be dire world consequences and there will be more famines and wars as a result because there won't be enough resources to cope with the population. My actual … well, what do I look forward to? I'm not really sure. I think life is well, such a broad, diverse activity that you know, you just don't know what's going to happen around the corner. So you know I'm looking forward to the rest of life, I think is probably what I'm looking forward to.

5   I agree that the biggest world scale problem is overpopulation and associated things. Well, such as the amount of cars trebling every five years, whatever it does. I don't think all the environmental problems are quite as severe as they're cracked up to be. I think most of those will sort themselves out, possibly. I'm also worried about unemployment … I don't think, I mean I'm worried about dying in a road accident because I've had several near crashes, well a couple actually. So I'm not sure what's going to happen in the next five years.

6   I don't know no I'd say if I was worried about anything in the future it would be about being embroiled in a third World War. Because I don't think that's completely out of the question.

7   I think the only thing I worry about is I don't like computers. They frighten me a lot. That really worries me. So … no one going out anywhere, just everything happening from a computer. But I think in general I'm not that worried. I think what I look forward to most is just being sort of by myself, not having to depend on anyone else. I'm really looking forward to that.

6 An imaginative projection into the future, giving students scope to think more deeply about their fears or their hopes about it.

> **OPTION**
>
> It is usually best to let imaginative ideas shape the structure, and not struggle to use rhyme or rhythm, which can distract from the emotional expression that is the main point of writing a poem.

7 After moving forward in time, students are asked to move backwards. The point of this is to promote oral exchanges between different generations and allow greater awareness of both the continuities and the differences in their experiences.

C PRIORITIES

1 A comparative exercise, this starts from the student's own priorities, moves to a comparison with those of others in the class, and finally, in the following exercise, offers a chance to compare with the results of a Europe-wide survey. Students write in their own scores, from 0 to 3. They then find the class average for each category by adding all the scores, then dividing by the number of people in the class. In larger classes, the average score can be calculated in groups first.

2 Ask students to write the article as though to be published for others in their school – or for the class or school newspaper, if there is one. They should try for an informative, journalistic style and register (an example is the short editorial in Exercise 3).

3 Students can read the article on their own first, noting any difficulties they have. They then read it with a partner and see whether they can resolve difficulties by guessing from context.

Language notes:
'gettalife' (slang) = 'get a life' is an instruction to people whose life is so full of work that they have no time to enjoy it
'workaholic' = a person addicted to work, on the model of 'alcoholic' = a person addicted to alcohol
'respondents' = people who have replied to a survey questionnaire
Several expressions are colourful metaphors which should be understandable through the context. Such are, for example, 'cracking under the stress' = becoming ill because of stress, and 'a time famine' = a very great need for more time.

The categorising activity which follows is a way of getting students to re-read the article and think about the dilemma between work and quality of life which it outlines.

ANSWERS

Life: rare moments; genuine living; fleeting seconds of quality time; away from the office or factory; personal commitments; time

Work: stressed workaholic; no life; cracking under the stress; work overload; staying in the office; time (time famine).

4 A brainstorming and prediction exercise, asking students to think imaginatively about the situation of people in full-time work, and what they wish for or regret. The lists on page 95 of the Student's Book confirm many of the ideas expressed in the editorial, highlighting once again lack of time as one of the great problems of contemporary life.

5 The extract which rounds off this part of the unit recycles some of the ideas that students have just been working with – the dilemma of people who work so hard in order to make money that they have no time to enjoy their lives. This time, it's a fictional teenager who describes these aspects in her father's lifestyle. The extract thus provides a bridge between the themes of part C and part D.

Students read the extract and respond to it with a partner, or with others in the class. Ask them to characterise the narrator, Gemma, and say what they think of her. She says she's 'flying', that is very happy, but it also means being 'high' on drugs. She compares her lifestyle favourably with that of other people, whose lives are built upon a deadening routine trying to acquire money and material goods. Her freedom is illusory, however, because the squatters do in fact need money, and many of them become slaves to their drug-taking habits.

Students are then asked to put themselves imaginatively into the position of Gemma's father. Encourage them to try to explore how he would justify his lifestyle, and how he would feel about his daughter's rejection of it. The letters can then be written as homework, to be discussed with others or displayed for comparison at the next class.

Notes about the author and novel:
Melvin Burgess was born in 1954 and was brought up in Sussex and Berkshire. After leaving school he moved to Bristol where he was generally unemployed, with occasional jobs mainly in the building industry. His first book, *The Cry of the Wolf,* was published in 1990. Melvin Burgess now writes full time and lives in Lancashire.

Junk (1996) was the winner of the Guardian Fiction Award and the Carnegie Medal. Although written as a novel for young people, its realistic portrayal of the dilemma of some adolescents today, and its vivid – sometimes horrifyingly vivid – style have won praise from readers of all ages.

Language notes:
The extract is in a teenager's slangy, colloquial spoken language.
'they've lost it' = they've lost their way in life, their life is meaningless
'he just burns himself out' = he wears himself out, becomes exhausted
'gotta' = renders the way 'got to' is often pronounced

PARENTS

A paired activity, in which each student reads one of the texts, makes notes on specific questions, and then discusses it with a partner. The two extracts show young people leading very different kinds of lives and having different relationships with their parents. After students have compared and talked about the literary texts, have a general class roundup of the main and most interesting points which came up in the discussion. Compare reactions to the two texts generally. Is there one which students in the class prefer?

Text A: This is another extract from the novel *Junk.* The events in it happen before the scene students have already read, when Gemma is still living at home. The conflict between Gemma and her parents shows the deteriorating relationship, which eventually pushes the girl to run away and become a squatter.

Language notes:

'all hell broke loose': a colloquial expression for 'conflict broke out'

'wagging': metaphorical expression for walking jerkily up and down

'this real beauty': colloquial and ironical for a stupid, absurd comment. Gemma considers that her father's concern about her 'reputation' is so old-fashioned that it seems to come from the Stone Age, so she replies sarcastically to it. Her sarcasm links GCEs, an academic qualification, with the ability to apply lipstick – that is to be 'feminine' in an old-fashioned way, to attract men.

GCE: this is what the father says in the text of the novel, though what he means is 'GCSE'. It is probable that irony is intended – the father is very positive about his daughter's educational achievements, but shows himself to be unaware of the exact name and nature of the exam in question!

Text B: Timberlake Wertenbaker's plays, produced at the Royal Court in London, have won high acclaim. *Our Country's Good,* based on Thomas Keneally's novel *The Playmaker,* and set in the early years of the British colonisation of Australia, won the Laurence Olivier Play of the Year Award in 1988. *Three Birds Alighting on A Field* won the Critics' Circle London Theatre Award for Best New Play, and the Writers' Guild Award for Best West End Play. The play is set in the London art world. Stephen is an embittered artist, struggling to make a living, resorting to commercial art work to support his family. Gwen has been to an expensive school but is shown in other parts of the scene to be rather ignorant. She exhibits the easy materialism of someone used to a fairly easy and even luxurious life.

ANSWERS

Possible answers to the first three questions

Junk. (characters) The father: hot-tempered, intolerant, authoritarian, old-fashioned in his views, sexist. The mother: loving but weak, subservient to the father. The daughter: headstrong, clever, rebellious, determined, sarcastic, flippant.

(relationships) The father seems determined to impose his will, while the mother seems more conciliatory. The daughter's relationship with the mother seems better than with the father.

(what each is trying to obtain) The father and mother are trying to restrain their daughter, prevent her from staying away at night, and get her to obey their rules of behaviour. The daughter is trying to get them to recognise her as an adult able to make her own rules.

Three Birds. (characters) The father: hard-working but weary, quite reasonable, down-to-earth, practical. The daughter: innocent, rather flighty, unrealistic, romantic, immature, dependent on her father, lacking in knowledge and experience of the world, selfish.

(relationships) The daughter still regards her father as a source of income, without considering whether he is able to provide; she does not yet see him as a person in his own right. The father seems wary of the daughter and her romantic fantasies.

(what each is trying to obtain) The daughter wants her father to fund her to go around the world; the father is trying to get her to adopt more realistic ambitions.

2 〔⚫⚫〕 A first listening, for gist only and an overall response. If your students find listening exercises difficult, give them the interviewer's first question: 'What do you think about the relations between you as a group of seventeen-year-olds, and your parents' generation?'

Ask them to predict the answers that could be given and put key words on the board. If they don't come up, add the following expressions which are central to what the Scottish students say:

a good relationship
reasonably friendly understanding
give and take (both sides are willing to make compromises)
same ideas
it just depends
the situation has got better
in some cases, pretty unreasonable and not really understanding

Language notes:
The interviewer uses the colloquial expression: 'understand where you're coming from?' An import from the USA, this is much used by young people to mean your situation and views.

TAPESCRIPT

Unit 10D, exercise 2. Five Scottish students talk about relations with parents.

I = Interviewer

I What do you think about the relationship between you as a group of seventeen-year-olds and your parents' generation?

Girl 1 I've got a very good relationship with my parents and if I want to go out and have a drink then they're usually OK with that, as long as I don't … you know there are sort of limits and I don't go … I don't do it too often so it gets to be a problem. And I don't I wouldn't take heavy drugs either, it's a sort of deal that we've got, so we've got a bit of give and take both ways.

I But with other people of your parents' generation, with teachers or whatever, do you think on the whole they understand where you're coming from?

Girl 2 Most of my friends' parents seem to … There are some cases when parents seem to be pretty unreasonable and not really understanding their kids' needs.

Girl 3 I think in the past few years the situation has got a bit better. Parents have decided, well this is what their children are like, this is the 90s as they say.

I So it's a reasonably friendly understanding kind of relationship, you reckon?

Boy 1 I reckon there has to be some sort of give and take, and there is … I've sort of reached a happy medium with them.

I It's not that you take and they give?

Boy 1 No, no, no. They've just sort of accepted it now, and so long as I don't go over the top they're pretty reasonable with me.

I Do you find the same thing?

Boy 2   With my mum personally, yeah, but I think it very much depends on the individuals. It's pretty impossible to generalise about like all people of my parents' age and all people of my age. I've got friends who have to do like all the housework around the house, look after themselves and be pretty much completely independent. I've got other friends who are more or less waited on hand and foot and have everything done for them. I've got friends who have been thrown out of the house and had to go and live with other – like, a friend of theirs. They didn't come to me fortunately. But I get on personally very well with my mum. And as far as age gap is concerned I think the 60s and 70s sounded like a pretty cool time. A lot of people seem to be copying them now, apart from anything, so I don't think there are that massive differences. We still have the same, like, ideas. Everybody's pretty much the same when they're a teenager. I mean there's obvious individual differences, but there's the same problems around every generation. So it just depends on what your parents are like and what you're like.

ANSWER

> On the whole, the students seem to have generally good relationships with their parents, although they know of others who don't.

3   ▭▭ A second listening, which aims for closer understanding of the opinions expressed, and invites students to respond. Students read the statements first, then listen to the recording. The discussion points have been structured so that your class can discuss the views of the students and give their own response without necessarily talking about their own relationships with their parents.

4   This exercise links the two halves of part D by comparing the views of the fictional characters and those of the Scottish students interviewed. This can lead to a more general discussion to summarise all the issues that have come up in the unit. If you know the class well and are confident that they are able to talk about themselves without embarrassment, a discussion of the recordings or the literary texts can open out into a comparison with the students' own experiences, and a reflection on cultural differences that might emerge.

ANSWERS

> One of the Scottish students mentions parents that are pretty unreasonable and not really understanding, which might be a parallel for Gemma's relationship with her parents. The fairly good relationship might be taken as close to Gwen's relationship, but the scene shows a lack of the 'give and take' that the Scottish students identify as necessary between children and parents. The Scottish students are aware of their parents' own generational issues (they mention the Sixties and Seventies), as opposed to Gemma, who thinks her father is 'Stone Age' in his views, and Gwen, who seems not to consider her father as a person at all.